PRAISE

"As a work of natural history, socio-economic history, and last but certainly not least gastronomic instruction, *Razor Clams* is a true delight. Well worth reading by anyone interested in its many-faceted narrative, it should be considered an absolutely essential book for those living on, near, or simply visiting the Pacific Northwest coast. But be advised—you won't be too long in reading it before a sudden craving for clam fritters or chowder takes hold." —*The Well-Read Naturalist*

"An entertaining account, and guide, to the real fun of digging your own food in the beach. . . . Berger's book is an excellent testimony that gathering is still an enriching, fun and tasty pursuit. Long may it be so." —*Cool Green Science*

"Written with verve, humor and well-researched fact . . . The book should become a go-to reference for razor clam enthusiasts, expert or casual." —*Everett Herald*

"*Razor Clams* appears to be, in fact, the only single tome that covers everything from history to how-tos. It includes chapters on ecology and anatomy, tribal treaties, clamming techniques for shovels versus tubes, and of course cooking tips and recipes." —*Daily World*

"This book is by far the quintessential guide to all things having to do with Pacific razor clams. . . . Not only does Berger go to great lengths to teach readers how to dig, clean, and prepare razor clams using his favorite recipes, but he also explores the commercial and recreational history of Northwest clamming." —*425 magazine*

"Berger's fun book blends hands-on natural and cultural history, his own experiences chasing clams . . . and a selection of recipes, from basic sauté options to chowders, ceviche and 'fresh clam balls.'" —*Cascadia Weekly*

RAZOR CLAMS

BURIED TREASURE of the PACIFIC NORTHWEST

DAVID BERGER

A RUTH KIRK BOOK

UNIVERSITY OF WASHINGTON PRESS
Seattle & London

Razor Clams was published with the assistance of a grant from the Ruth Kirk Book Fund, which supports publications that inform the general public on the history, natural history, archaeology, and Native cultures of the Pacific Northwest.

This book was also supported by the Northwest Writers Fund, which promotes the work of some of the region's most talented nonfiction writers and was established through generous gifts from Linda and Peter Capell, Janet and John Creighton, Michael J. Repass, and other donors.

Copyright © 2017 by David Berger
First paperback edition 2019
Printed and bound in the United States of America
Design and cover illustration by Andrew Brozyna
Composed in Adobe Garamond
22 21 20 19   5 4 3 2 1

All rights reserved. No part of this publication may be reproduced or transmitted in any form or by any means, electronic or mechanical, including photocopy, recording, or any information storage or retrieval system, without permission in writing from the publisher.

Unless otherwise noted, photographs and drawings are courtesy of the author.

UNIVERSITY OF WASHINGTON PRESS
www.washington.edu/uwpress

LIBRARY OF CONGRESS CATALOGING-IN-PUBLICATION DATA
Names: Berger, David, author.
Title: Razor clams : buried treasure of the Pacific Northwest / David Berger.
Description: Seattle : University of Washington Press, 2017. | Series: A Ruth Kirk book | Includes bibliographical references and index. | Description based on print version record and CIP data provided by publisher; resource not viewed.
Identifiers: LCCN 2017007244 (print) | LCCN 2017011770 (ebook) | ISBN 9780295741437 (ebook) | ISBN 9780295741420 (hardcover : acid-free paper)
Subjects: LCSH: Clamming—Washington (State) | Razor clams—Washington (State) | Beaches—Washington (State) | Berger, David—Travel—Washington (State) | Washington (State)—Social life and customs. | Washington (State)—Description and travel.
Classification: LCC SH400.5.C53 (ebook) | LCC SH400.5.C53 B47 2017 (print) | DDC 639/.4409797—dc23
LC record available at https://lccn.loc.gov/2017007244

ISBN (paperback): 978-0-295-74544-2

The paper used in this publication is acid-free and meets the minimum requirements of American National Standard for Information Sciences—Permanence of Paper for Printed Library Materials, ANSI Z 39.48–1984. ∞

*To my parents, to whom I owe so much,
and to my wife, Karen, the big clam in my life*

Heaven is under our feet as well as over our heads.
—HENRY DAVID THOREAU

CONTENTS

CHAPTER 1	Introductions	9
CHAPTER 2	Lay of the Land: Long Beach and Ocean Shores	24
CHAPTER 3	Sacred Treaties	41
CHAPTER 4	Ecology and Anatomy	55
CHAPTER 5	Past Abundances	74
CHAPTER 6	The Era of NIX and Domoic Acid	89
CHAPTER 7	Pumping and Counting	109
CHAPTER 8	Licensed to Carry	127
CHAPTER 9	Eating Them, After All, Is the Point	146
CHAPTER 10	Will's First Clam	162
CODA	Practical Matters	171
APPENDIX 1	Washington State Razor Clam Personal Use Regulations, 1929–2015	185
APPENDIX 2	Recreational Razor Clam License Information in Washington, 1982–1993	187
LIST OF RECIPES		191
NOTES		193
SELECTED BIBLIOGRAPHY		211
INDEX		215
ACKNOWLEDGMENTS		221

CHAPTER 1

INTRODUCTIONS

THE state has confirmed a spring razor clamming opening, so I immediately telephone my wife. "Skip work. There are some great low tides coming up." The tide chart shows minus tides the third week of April, extending through the weekend and into the week—big lows that promise to expose many feet of intertidal beach and thus good razor clamming.

I call the small motel we like. Fortunately, they have room. The motel books up quickly during the days of minus tides, in the spring, when the dig is on. We arrive in late afternoon. The surf rumbles steadily. The beach is so flat that the breaking waves glide up the sand for a hundred and fifty feet, tapering to the gentlest lap. The next morning we awake and slip from the motel bed onto the cold floor. The weather has changed; the sky is dark and threatening. Karen drinks her coffee and dresses. She puts on rain pants and jacket, and shiny black milking boots, and ties her hood tightly. She is fully encased in rubber and no doubt will float like a buoy if the need arises.

We drive to the beach and the moment we open the car door the wind blasts our faces, blowing in hard from across the Pacific with nothing at all to obstruct it. It's raining intermittently, and dampness seeps into every crevice. Nevertheless, there are hundreds of people around us, all gathered for this singular purpose. It's an hour before low tide. Some people bang the beach, prospecting for clams, and a few dig, but most are waiting for the waters to lower and expose the prime habitat. My hands are freezing. I keep them in my pockets. The sun is up but barely lights the beach. It's tempting just to quit. But nobody does. Clumps of people extend up and down the beach as far as the eye can see, facing the sea like a line of Roman legionnaires.

The tide continues to drop. The waters are receding, exposing the intertidal zone where the razor clams live. Suddenly, people are digging everywhere, as if given some invisible signal. The line of people advances and attacks. Cold hands and wet feet are forgotten.

I look for clams at the water's edge. A wave breaks and I brace myself. Dark water, pieces of shell, and pebbles swirl around my ankles. In difficult conditions like this, when the clams aren't apparent, it helps to prospect—banging the beach with the shovel. The vibration can cause a gurgling spurt: a show. I smack till my forearms hurt, but nothing. Finally, a spurt. I place the shovel behind the little dimple that results and, with a few pulls, excavate a narrow hole. I see the clam's pale neck telescoping down into the sand. I dig after it with my bare hands, following the hole it leaves behind. Damn, these clams can move fast! My arm is deep into the beach when my fingers touch the shell and pull it up. It's a hefty clam, glossy, tapered, and as elegant as a 1920s cigarette case. I wash it off in a puddle of water and add it to the net hanging off my belt.

I walk up the beach to the drier sand to find Karen, who is digging with an aluminum tube. This is a cylinder about thirty inches long, with a crosspiece handle at the top. It's an effective tool, especially in drier sand. Karen has only a few clams, but they're large.

"I'm wiped out," she says. "I've dug a lot of holes."

"You didn't get a clam each time?" I ask.

"No, maybe every other hole," she says.

You can dig a lot of holes while clamming, each one teaching you about water and sand, their endless interactions and significant weight.

Black clouds rumble on top of us from down the beach. We are swallowed by darkness. Only people immediately adjacent are visible. Suddenly hail comes whistling out of the sky. We huddle with our backs to the weather. The hail bounces and the beach turns white, layered with pellets. Then it stops and the cloud continues up the beach.

Karen spots a dimple she thinks is a clam, rocks the tube deep into the beach, and grunts up a column of sand. She rests while I poke through the sand, and there's the clam. She puts it in her net.

The low tide is over and the sea is flooding in again, smoothing over the mounds of sand and filling in holes. People are dispersing, returning from whence they came. Not that many have their limits, due to the conditions. This was a hard dig. Some have just a few clams. Karen and I are each one short of our limit, fourteen clams instead of fifteen, but we're weary. My hands are aching and I can hardly clasp the shovel as we walk up the beach to the car.

Later in the afternoon the sun comes out and everything glows warm and cheerful. At the motel's outdoor cleaning station, I dip a colander with razor clams into a pot of simmering water. The shells spring open and the razor clam flesh spills out. Dipping, first step in cleaning the clams. I dump the opened clams into a sinkful of cold water to stop any possible cooking.

A fellow walks in from the beach and lays his clams on a screened table to hose off sand. I glance at his haul. Fifteen clams, all large, not a single one broken. A pro. The stout woman across from me whose hands haven't stopped working puts down her knife, picks up a pair of scissors, and starts cutting out the fat clam stomachs and other dark, inedible parts.

"I think I'll make some chowder tonight," she says.

I'm cleaning clams, too, and the piles of clam meat are growing. I admire the clam's construction, as I always do: a cathedral of siphons and tubes. The garbage pail fills with discarded shells, lustrous purple and white inside. I prop one of the shells upright on the counter while I clean. I'll take it home, along with a few others. In a few months it will dry up, become bleached and fragile. But for now the thin shell is fresh and supple, and the perfectly symmetrical oblongs look like angel wings, with a drop of mother of pearl at the hinge.

Early evening and we prepare dinner. We sauté the clams with shallots, oil, and lots of butter. We reward ourselves by cooking mostly the tender feet. We butterfly them, and each side is laden with spawn, the clam's reproductive material, a.k.a. clam butter. We cook them for a minute or so on each side. It isn't long till there's a big platter on the table. The razor clams are fresh, the taste sweet and distinctive, and we dip crusty bread into the butter to soak up the razor clam flavor. We hum with delight.

I first went razor clamming out of the most casual curiosity. I was a transplant from the East to the West Coast. I'd barely heard of razor clams, but I had a clam shovel I'd purchased at a garage sale, thinking it might be useful in the garden. I somehow managed to get myself to the beach at the right time. I can't remember much about the one and only clam I caught. I was too spent from battling surf and sand. The clam was much deeper in the beach than I had expected, and it moved fast. Subsequently, I heard people say: "These are clams you have to chase! It's sport!" But nobody had told me that. To find myself on a miles-long beach, under an endless sky, chasing a clam buried in the sand, was quite novel. After hours of fruitless effort, I found the one clam only after extending my arm much farther into the sand than I thought sensible; I was up to my shoulder in the beach and felt like I was reaching in to turn around a breached calf. But then my fingertips brushed the tip of something hard. I pinched and gave a pull. The object, to my surprise, pulled downward. I pinched harder

A razor clamming dig can bring out many people.

and pulled upward. The clam strained and pulled downward. It was a battle of strength and wills that I only slowly won.

I wasn't alone that first dig, one arm deep in the beach, pinching and pulling for all I was worth. As I discovered, many people love to dig and eat the Pacific razor clam. The whole tribe of society gathers to dig its allotted fifteen clams. Old-timers. Hipsters. Families with dogs. Groups of twentysomethings. Sportsmen in camouflage clothes. Mothers pushing strollers. Busy urbanites and coastal denizens. Even couples on dates, sweetly murmuring. When I arrived at the beach, I saw the entire arc of humanity lined up in front of the surf. I was stunned. On a good clamming weekend, people flood from every corner of Washington, Oregon, and points beyond. It is really the quintessential Northwest activity. Salmon, move over. A mass of humanity comes to the shore to chase, catch, clean, cook, and consume this seafood delicacy. There is joy in the abundance. It's a family activity and the lore is often handed down generationally. It's not uncommon to see eighty-year-olds, male and female, out on the beach pursuing an activity that they learned as kids. No child forgets the wonder of being on the beach, digging for clams with a throng of gyrating humanity, and no octogenarian either.

One season, after a dig, I fell in love with razor clams. I became infatuated; they were all I could think of, day and night. It was a one-sided love affair, what with me mooning around and the razor clams going about their business as if I didn't exist. I explained to a friend that I had fallen in love, had held a clam my hand and felt an ache in my heart, and she looked at me strangely.

The state of affairs came upon me without warning. I was cleaning a limit at an outdoor station specifically designed for the purpose—essentially some sinks and counter space, and a pot for dipping. I was alone; my fellow clammers had come and gone. I could hear the white noise of the Pacific Ocean in the distance. The sweet smell from scores of cleaned clams hung heavy in the air. I laid out a clam the size of my palm on a wooden board. I was cutting away the shell and viscera when all at once the entirety of razor clamming suffused my being. The big sky, the closeness to nature, the fellowship with other clammers, the tasty meal, the physical challenge all crowded in. But it was the single quivering clam that most occupied me. Each element of it seemed perfect. I became enamored of the long neck, the powerful foot, the translucent oblong body. It was all perfect, I thought, as I peered at the clam and cradled it in my palm. I noticed how the tip of the foot was hard and pointed, how the foot curled and rippled with power. I noticed how the clam body nestled in the clam shell, the muscles levering against the thin shell's reinforcing rib. I was smitten by the streamlined geometry of the shell, the outer surface lacquered and smooth.

Even though enamored, I also had to laugh. The neck extended like a slinky. The single foot somehow resembled both a baby's leg and an elephant's haunch. The razor clam was a cathedral of engineering, but to us humans, who have two of most everything and for whom symmetry is so important, it also appears comical. One plump pogo stick of a leg. A neck with no head. My funny valentine indeed. Nonetheless, it was perfect. When the shell opened, in the process of cleaning, the two halves unfolded at the hinge. Inside, the shell was pearly white with blushes of purple and pink. The interior lines radiated like light, and I couldn't help feeling an archetypal resonance—that the clam was snug in a kind of celestial shawl.

It had rained heavily earlier in the morning, but now the sun was out and the earth was steaming as I held the wiggling clam in my hand. I looked at the confabulation of siphons, filters, organs, neck, and foot. I thought of the clams in the dark depths of the beach, the sand pressing in steady as a mother's hug. I was glad to be alone in the clam kitchen with these strange feelings, with just the natural world for company. I recognized them as peculiar. Clams are not a typical object of the heart. And yet I felt that kind of yearning.

Eventually I sought a more formal introduction to *Siliqua patula*, or the Pacific razor clam, as it's commonly known. It dwells only on the western edge of the North American continent, from northern California to southern Alaska, but most especially on the fifty-three miles of flat, sandy beaches that make up Washington's southern coast, prime habitat for razor clams. Here, they are plentiful in numbers hard to imagine.

The shell is an elegant affair that grows to about 6.25 inches long at full maturity. It fits in your hand just so, elongated and oblong, the exterior shiny and in shades of golden brown, olive, and tan. It's a streamlined, wily creature designed to move up and down in the sand column, like a little elevator. The clam's digging foot extends from the bottom, and its siphon—or neck, as it's commonly called—extends from the top. The neck, the only part of the clam to poke above the sand, is tough as tire rubber. The body is a pouch of soft viscera, encased by the mantle that builds the shell, and enfolded by skirts and fringes. The foot is muscular and holds the reproductive tissue, ironic since this is the least suggestive part of the clam, neither phallic like the long neck nor vulvate like the body fringes. These metaphorical parts are understated and in perfect balance, as if the clam were a cosmopolitan hermaphrodite.

Most of the time the neck and the foot protrude from the shell, forming a distinctive profile, though the foot can retract all the way into the shell and the neck can retract most of the way, like that of a turtle. The shell, however, is always somewhat agape, and the animal is visible all around except at the hinge. The clam doesn't so much inhabit the shell as wear it like fashionable light armor.

And then there are the missing parts. No teeth or barbs, no poison or claws. No weapons. Only a strong foot for fleeing. The clam is a pacifist.

Both the Pacific razor clam and the Atlantic razor clam (*Ensis directus*), found on the East Coast, are commonly called razor clams, but the two are different genera and have a different shape. The shell of *Ensis directus* really does look like an old-fashioned straight-edge razor, narrow and thin, or a jackknife, per its other common name, Atlantic jackknife clam. The Pacific razor clam is bigger and heavier, with an oval silhouette. Whether its common name derives from a general resemblance to many other clams around the world that are commonly called razor clams, or from the thin edges that can gash unwary fingers, is ambiguous. But certainly diggers need to be careful, as many a neophyte with a scar can attest. The scientific name derives from the clam's appearance—*siliqua* being Latin for "pod" and *patula* for "open" or "gaping."

Over time, I started razor clamming more frequently and began daydreaming about the activity. I imagined a spring opener in morning sun, and an evening dig with folks looking for clam shows by lantern and headlamp. I found it reassuring to recall this world existing seemingly out of time and place. When I saw shells from previous digs around the house, I remembered that the surf was steadily roaring at the coast, and a multitude of razor clams were living out their lives in a great city in the sand, even as I was living out mine.

Their city is invisible, of course, and when you arrive at the beach to take stock only an expanse of ocean and sky is to be seen, a vast diorama of light. An untold number of razor clams, perhaps the best eating clam

Siliqua patula, the Pacific razor clam

in the world, lie buried in the sand, each precisely hunched over, hinge facing toward the sea. But a casual visitor would not suspect there's even a one. And when visitors stumble on a horde of people tearing up the beach like mad gophers, they are amazed. In fact, a significant percentage of Washington's population has joined the razor clamming ranks over the decades, especially as the country became more mobile after World War II, and left gas rationing and bad memories behind. Some years have seen nearly one million digger trips—that is, a million discrete trips to the ocean shore to hunt for razor clams. People discover the activity, taste the primal joy of abundance, and invite family and friends on a regular basis. During a recent season, people harvested more than six million clams, enough to pile a hundred clams on every seat in the Seattle Seahawks' football stadium. It's not too unusual for folks to display some razor clam shells at home or in the garage as trophies, or to read in a coastal newspaper obituary, "So-and-so loved to razor clam and took pride in always getting a limit."

The phenomenon thrives despite the proliferation of video games and computer screens, cable television and professional sports. A turn away from nature? Not to the men, women, and children who flock to the coast to clam. Electronics die a quick death next to sand and salt water, as do quotidian worries. Sea, sky, and razor clam shows leave little room for other thoughts. The beach is wild, the undertaking elemental. It's challenging, and yet most who try meet with success. Razor clamming is the people's activity, an often-ritualized experience enjoyed over and over. You dig with shovel and tube, and hands. You perch on the coastal rim where sand, sky, sun, and water edge together. You brave the elements and accompany the clams on the rough journey from this special place to foodstuff. You know where your dinner comes from; you harvested it just a few hours before.

Razor clamming has evolved—in the early years, clams were commercially canned, for example, and the resource has had its ups and downs—but it's always been shovel and sand, digger and quarry, one clam at a time, mano a mano. Razor clamming is part of the psychic bedrock, and its hold on the region is strong. If the season gets curtailed or canceled, as occasionally happens due to lack of clams or health advisories, people are perturbed. You might as well cancel Christmas! And when there are many clamming days, and the clams are numerous and good sized, people are happy.

Of course, abundance isn't the only consideration shaping the experience. State authorities declare when and how many clams can be caught, and those regulations influence the razor clamming phenomenon. Having a dig around New Year's Day in January practically created a new holiday for aficionados. Weather is a defining issue when you are going to be in it, and summer digs have been off limits since 1973, pushing razor clammers into less hospitable seasons for the sake of protecting baby clams and summer tourists, and enhancing year-round coastal visitation.

But, seasons and regulations aside, the bar to entry to razor clamming is low. You use a shovel—preferably with a narrow blade—or

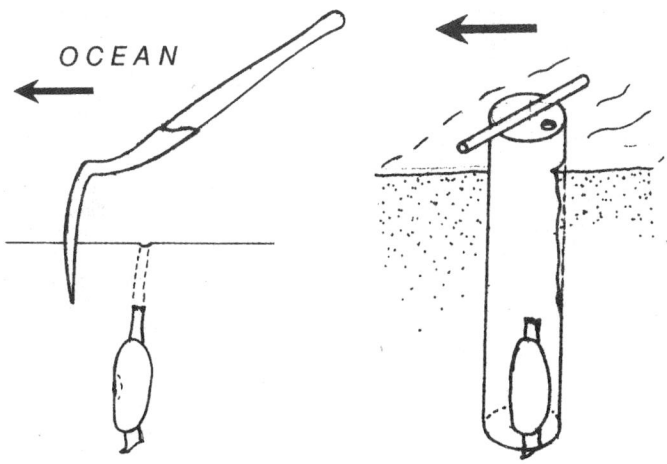

(LEFT) The clam shovel is placed four to six inches seaward of the clam show, with blade vertical. (RIGHT) The clam tube is placed over the clam show, slanting away from the ocean, and rocked or twisted into the sand. Courtesy Washington Department of Fish and Wildlife (WDFW).

a tube, a simple cylinder made of metal or plastic with a handle that creates a partial vacuum to lift up a column of sand. Most people think the tube is easier than the shovel, though it can take time to gain finesse with whatever tool you are using. A bucket or net for holding the catch completes the gear. My wife's uncle used a bleach bottle with a window cut out, which he tied to his belt with a shoelace. When he became too infirm to razor clam, he passed it along to us.

Once you have your gear—shovel or tube, and bucket or net—you have to go to the ocean at low tide. That's when the receding water reveals the intertidal sand in which the clams live. There are two low and two high tides every day on the Northwest coast, six hours apart. On the East Coast, each tide is about the same elevation, but on the West Coast, one high tide is higher than the other, and one low tide is lower. Those lower low tides are when clammers flock to the beach.

Once you make it to a low tide, you have to ignore the expansive sky, the sandy beaches that go on for miles, and the Pacific Ocean extending flat in front of you all the way to the horizon. You have to concentrate instead on the grains of sand right at your feet. You study one little section of sand, then another. Everything else drops away. You see the ripples of sand left by receding water, and perhaps a piece of sand dollar. And then you spot a hole, or a dimple, or some other show. You dig quickly, lest the surf wash the show from sight, and then lest the clam escape into the depths of the sand. When done with the day's tide, if you're fortunate, your net bulges with golden-brown clams. Then it's on to cleaning them. Perhaps you'll wonder how the clams manage to burrow about as fast as you can dig for them, and why sometimes you find so many and other times none at all. Over the decades, I have had many such questions about these creatures that are so different from we humans and other mammals. My misconceptions were many. But I knew the razor clam phenomenon was as real as the coastal rain and pointy evergreen trees, attracting a multitude who love being on the beach, digging in the briny ocean wetness, securing a foodstuff from the wild, feeling the glory of abundance, and holding aloft each clam dug from the sand as if it were the Golden Fleece itself.

BASIC SAUTÉED RAZOR CLAMS
Makes 2 servings

When it comes to razor clams, one of my obsessions is cooking time, and not overcooking the clams lest they become tough and chewy. They really can cook quickly—almost instantly. Even Ivar's "acres of clams" restaurant, the archetypal Northwest seafood establishment, warned when fried razor clams were on the menu in the 1960s that they were "tasty, but may be tough." But people have different opinions as to when a razor clam is ready to eat, as Karen reminds me when I hover while she is in front of the frying pan.

"Karen, those clams are cooked! Take them out!"

"No, give them just a few seconds more."

Some diggers like to show off their prowess by cleaning clams so precisely that neck, digger, and mantle all stay together. The whole clam makes a nice presentation, certainly. But I prefer to separate the parts for cooking. Fat diggers go in first, then necks, and finally the thin mantle, and the pieces can be removed when just cooked.

This recipe and the two that follow are simple sautés. This one contains just butter and clams. The second has a brown butter sauce with some shallots and lemon juice, and the third is with capers and white wine.

 1 teaspoon vegetable oil
 1½ tablespoons unsalted butter
 4 to 6 razor clams (optionally separated into necks and diggers, cut into pieces if large)
 Salt and freshly ground black pepper

 Baguette, for serving

In a large frying pan, heat the oil and butter over medium-high heat. Add the clams without overcrowding (cook them in two batches, if necessary). Cook about 1 to 2 minutes on each side, or until just starting to firm. Remove smaller clams or pieces as they are cooked. Add salt and pepper to taste. Serve the clams in the skillet, or cut into pieces with kitchen scissors and serve on plates drizzled with pan butter, with extra pan butter in a small bowl for dipping. Serve with the baguette.

SAUTÉED RAZOR CLAMS IN BROWN BUTTER
Makes 2 servings

- 3 tablespoons unsalted butter
- 2 teaspoons finely chopped shallots
- ½ teaspoon minced fresh thyme
- 4 to 6 razor clams (optionally separated into necks and diggers, cut into pieces if large)
- ½ teaspoon fresh lemon juice
- **Salt and freshly ground black pepper**

In a large frying pan, heat the butter over medium-high heat. Just as the milk solids in the butter begin to brown, add the shallots. Cook until the butter is brown and the shallots have softened. Add the thyme, stir, and then add the clams. Cook, turning once and spooning butter over the clams, for 1 to 2 minutes, or just starting to firm. Remove the clams. Let the sauce cool slightly, then add the lemon juice and salt and pepper to taste. Serve the clams in a puddle of brown butter, or with the brown butter in a small bowl on the side for dipping.

SAUTÉED RAZOR CLAMS WITH CAPERS
Makes 2 servings

- 1 cup dry white wine
- 2 tablespoons unsalted butter
- 1 tablespoon olive or vegetable oil
- 2 tablespoons minced shallots
- 2½ tablespoons capers, rinsed
- 1 clove garlic, thinly sliced
- 4 to 6 razor clams (optionally separated into necks and diggers, cut into pieces if large)

Salt
Lemon, for squeezing
Chopped parsley or basil, for garnish

Pour the wine into a large skillet and cook over medium-high heat until reduced by half, about 4 to 5 minutes. Add the butter, oil, shallots, capers, and garlic, reduce the heat to medium, and cook for 2 more minutes. Add the clams and cook about 20 seconds, then remove the skillet from the heat and cover. Allow to sit while the clams continue to gently cook from the residual heat, for a couple of minutes. Taste the sauce and add salt, if needed, and a squeeze or two of lemon juice if it needs brightening. Garnish with the parsley.

CHAPTER 2

LAY OF THE LAND
Long Beach and Ocean Shores

THE car was loaded down with shovel, clam tubes, waders, and cooler. Nothing was packed, just thrown in the back. I was headed to the city of Long Beach, one of several prime razor clamming locations in the state of Washington. Long Beach had resurrected its razor clam festival after many decades and was dedicating its newly refurbished twelve-foot-tall razor clam sculpture. Plus, the weekend promised good minus tides for clamming. All excellent reasons to visit the city and the Long Beach Peninsula, a sliver of sandy land near the Columbia River that stretches due north into the ocean like a finger, one side facing the restless Pacific Ocean and the other the quiet mudflats of Willapa Bay.

It's all about water here on the coast, and to emphasize that fact the rain was pummeling down. It made me pessimistic for the clamming ahead. The frequent wet in the non-summer months helps account for the lichen-draped trees and cranberry farms. When Meriwether Lewis and William Clark first came down the Columbia River and arrived at the Pacific Ocean, not far from Long Beach, in early November 1805, Clark famously wrote, "Ocian in view O! The joy." But his happiness was soon tempered by the "rain falling in torrents." When the rain falls without mercy or the gray skies press

Spurting razor clam sculpture and oversized skillet in the city of Long Beach. The clam spurts on the hour.

down like a heavy quilt you appreciate the hardy quality of the people who live here year after year.

One of those hardy souls is Bob Andrew, mayor of Long Beach since 2008. It's a part-time job, and most weeks Andrew is up at 2 a.m. making cookies and bread at his bakery. Tourism is the lifeblood of the peninsula, and the city of Long Beach is the heart, with cheerful storefronts and quirky landmarks. The mayor told me the city was originally called Tinkerville, after Henry Tinker, who founded the city and had the original vision of Long Beach as a seaside tourist attraction. Like many locals, the mayor is full of regional history and lore. It's as if the very tenuousness of the peninsula—a spit, really, and an accident of Columbia River sediments and ocean currents—creates a need to put down other roots. Beaches grow or shrink. Water rises, seeps, and covers roads during heavy rains. The wind is almost always pushing and jabbing. And everybody nowadays knows about the sword of Damocles just fifty miles offshore, where the Juan de Fuca oceanic plate thrusts under the North American continental plate, sticking and causing the earth to rise and move a quarter to a half inch every year, like some poor prisoner on the rack. Seismologists say that the Cascadia subduction zone has brought major earthquakes and tsunamis to the area every 250 to 600 years, on average. The last major event was in 1700. Tsunami warning signs are everywhere, depicted by a human figure chased by what looks like a circular saw blade. Evacuation route arrows point to higher ground, though there's precious little of it around. Remembering genealogies and history can be a comfort amid such dynamic circumstances.

Mayor Andrew has his own particular history on the peninsula. His dad built a cottage retreat out of salvaged wood that they shared with another family. Andrew would play in the dunes and on the beach, and fish for perch and hoagies. Offshore he could still see masts of the wrecked ship *The Alice*, buried upright in the sand and shallow water. No fancy vacation, but a version of paradise just the same. Razor clamming was a group effort. Between the two families, they would gather eleven limits of clams, twenty-four clams each at that time. They'd clean the 264 clams on a production line. The dads dipped the shells in hot water so the shells would spring open and the clam bodies would spill out. The kids cleaned out the sand while the moms removed the little dark parts from the digger. They ground the necks for chowder, fried up the diggers to eat, and canned the rest. The tough tips of the neck were saved for baiting hooks and fishing in the surf. It was a sequence of activities—digging, cleaning, frying, fishing—still done today by many.

The original Long Beach Razor Clam Festival started in 1940 as a way to attract visitors. The small city had a parade, and promoters dreamed up the idea of cooking a giant clam fritter. The first year they borrowed a pan, but the next year they commissioned their own, some fifteen feet from base to handle. The "world's largest" iron skillet toured Washington and Oregon in 1948 strapped onto a pickup truck, the handle extending out over the front bumper. It was accompanied by clam queens wearing razor clamshell–adorned swimsuits and an entourage of cars, some with wooden razor clam sculptures strapped to their roofs.

Though the festival petered out, Long Beach never forgot about its extravaganza. Decades later, in 1994, city officials retrieved the pan

The Long Beach Razor Clam Festival in 1940. Cooking the "world's largest clam fritter" required two hundred pounds of razor clams and twenty dozen eggs. The festival started in 1940 and stopped a few years after World War II. Courtesy Pacific Shellfish Ephemera, Matt Winters Digital Collection

and repaired the rusted bottom with fiberglass. Doing so rendered it useless as cookware, but displayed upright in downtown Long Beach in a courtyard it became a favorite photo stop for tourists. And in 2013 volunteers and the city brought back the festival; the following year they revived the fritter cooking event as well, this time as a culinary competition. The question was what to use for a frying pan. Someone recalled that the city had made a welded aluminum pan in 1994 to cook elephant ears for the dedication of Main Street, the same year it had repaired the original iron one. Sure enough, the pan existed, stored upside down and doing duty outside as an occasional stage. (Long Beach has an on-again, off-again relationship with oversized cookware.)

The aluminum pan was more tub than winsome skillet, but it would do. Rather than making one giant fritter, as had been done decades earlier, each team from the local high school's culinary arts program made individual fritters according to their own gourmet recipes. The

Long Beach resurrected its razor clam festival in 2013 after it had been defunct for more than sixty years.

jet burners were lit. The cooking oil poured in. The teens worked with concentration under the red-and-white tent despite the festival crowds just a few feet away.

Later in the afternoon, after the competition concluded and the winners were announced, Mayor Andrew, in waders and boots—he'd gone clamming in the morning—rededicated the twelve-foot-tall razor clam sculpture, whose mechanism had been restored to spurt water on the hour or by insertion of a quarter. The clam shares a corner of the city with the original "world's largest fry pan." Together, the two look like oversized charms, escapees from a giant Monopoly set. Their dollhouse appeal is irresistible. Oddly enough, no one at the city knows who made the clam sculpture or how it came to be; it's just there, much like the razor clams themselves in the beach a short distance away.

The mayor said a few words, and the weekend continued with a chowder contest and razor clam digging lessons. I continued with more razor clamming. My first dig had been on a Thursday morning. I'd been surprised to find myself in a long queue of cars on the way to the beach, since it was a weekday. Our caravan headed north past closely spaced beach cottages. We all turned onto the Ocean Park beach access road and then we were on the beach. 7:03 a.m. Low tide was not until 8:40. It was hard going and took a lot of prospecting, but I dug a limit.

"How'd you do?" asked Ray, the proprietor back at my motel.

"A limit," I said. "Really fat, healthy-looking clams. But they were deep. Really deep."

"That's the storm passing through," he said. "The clams go deep."

My second dig, I returned to the same spot. There was wind somewhere offshore and the surf was chaotic, the color of peat moss. I could see that nets were empty. Folks looked discouraged, and no wonder. It was only twenty minutes till the low and nets should have been filling. Instead, people were just standing around. The clams were holed up but good. There weren't many people about; most had left or exercised the good sense to stay home. I was standing in the water in waders when several waves sallied in from different directions, and though I was braced, suddenly I was bouncing along the sandy bottom. How could I have forgotten the strength of the sea? The wave knocked down a gang of us. We clutched our clamming gear and rolled along. Finally, I managed to get to my feet.

"Are you okay, Grandma?" I heard a young man say.

"You just have to relax," she said to her grandson, to me, to the sky, grinning to beat the band. "Nothing you can do."

You can bet for the rest of the morning we were wary. When we saw a large wave coming in, we ran like the dickens up the beach, nets and shovels clanging, till it eddied around our ankles harmlessly. We were just like the sandpipers, following the surf down on little stilt feet, then hurrying back when the waves and water started swishing in. Up and down the beach we went, banging and scurrying. As my friend Harvey likes to say, you haven't been razor clamming till a wave washes over your shoulder. It's a joke because he is talking about those times when you are kneeling down on the beach by the surf, reaching in for a clam, and an incoming wave washes over you and you just hold onto the clam, biding your time till the water recedes. It can take minutes. Water rolls up a long way on a flat beach and takes its own sweet time draining back. But sometimes you can be standing upright one moment and knocked down into the water the next.

My final dig, the sun was shining and the surf was calm as glass. That's the coast in spring. The weather is always changing. The light was perfect for spotting clam shows, which were everywhere. I took my time and was about the last person on the beach when a beater Ford sedan pulled up. The driver rolled down the window.

"Are they jumping in the net?" he asked.

"Yeah, pretty much," I said.

The driver was as weather-beaten as the low pine trees off in the dunes. He was wearing a baseball cap with a feather, and a little braid sneaked out the back. Native American, I thought, which he later confirmed. He got out of the car and we talked a while. He lived not far from the beach and owned property. He'd grown up right here at the northern end of the peninsula. He told me about buying his clam license in the city of Long Beach, down the road a few miles, and he talked about it like it was a trip to a foreign country. He told me stories of the old days, when he'd worked at a cannery, and his wife used to clean people's clams. Forty cents to clean a limit. He still had the sign. She'd died the previous Thanksgiving. They were married forty-five years, he said, and she had died in his arms.

I watched him clam, the sun illuminating everything with a warm tinge; it was so late in the tide that no one else was at the beach. Just one old guy with a shovel, framed by the blue sky and distant horizon, smartly digging despite his age. The beach is in motion all the time, changing minute by minute. But it also seems to be just the same, and his classic razor clamming posture—leaning over the shovel, one knee bent—seemed as eternal as the wind, surf, and dunes.

That was a memorable day. Good weather, and the clams jumped in the net.

A hundred-mile drive north of Long Beach, after circumventing the watery obstacles of Grays Harbor and Willapa Bay, is the city of Ocean Shores. Like Long Beach, it is a classic razor clamming destination. It too has a razor clam festival, and at one time it had an iconic razor clam sculpture as well. Ocean Shores sprang into existence in 1960 as a planned community offering the recreational fruits of the region: fishing, hunting, golfing, beachcombing, and, of course, razor clamming. The developers bought a cattle ranch perched by the ocean and Grays Harbor, then platted it into 12,000 tightly packed lots, scraping and dredging the sand, salt marsh, forest, and accreted tideland in a way that would never be allowed today.

Ocean Shores lots sold quickly, thanks to aggressive marketing that sold a vision of paradise for ordinary working-class folks. An eight-foot-tall razor clam sculpture carved from a hunk of wood stood in front of the Executive Villa sales office. New property owners would sometimes pose for pictures clutching title papers. The sculpture was well proportioned and faithfully captured the clam's shape and appearance, even including growth rings on the shell. But, as photographs reveal, the sculpture had a prominent anatomical mistake: the clam's foot was pointed the wrong way. That is, the toe—the pointed end of the foot—faced toward the front of the clam, instead of toward the back, the hinge side.

This error was not an isolated mistake. It's a curious fact that, even with countless thousands of clams nearby to serve as models, representations of the razor clam are often anatomically incorrect in this way. Apparently no one noticed, or at least commented, on the sculpture's error.

I suppose the misstep could be explained as the artist's need to better support the object's substantial mass. In fact, though, the error is everywhere, in two-dimensional as well as three-dimensional representations, and it betrays the tyranny of preconceptions. We simply impose our understanding of the human form onto the clam. Toes and feet face front. It just looks right. Even if it's just one toe and one foot. (The spurting sculpture at Long Beach avoids the issue entirely by slicing off the bottom of the clam, with the clam upright on a concrete base. No foot depicted.)

One dark night in December 1971, Ocean Shores' massive razor clam sculpture disappeared. An inebriated city crew used heavy equipment to nab the sculpture and bury it somewhere nearby, or so the leading speculation goes. Maybe the holiday-season pranksters wanted to return the clam to its rightful home in the sand, or, who knows, were perturbed by its anatomical inaccuracy. The local newspaper joked that a future archeologist might uncover the clam and wonder if the local people worshipped razor clams, adding that the speculation "wouldn't be far off."

Everybody expected the sculpture to be returned quickly, but it never was. As late as 2009, forty years on, a city councilman expressed hope that it would come back so it could be placed at the center of a soon-to-be-built roundabout. But it has not reappeared. No one has ever confessed. The whodunit remains unsolved.

By the 1970s, developers were feuding, financial shenanigans had caused scandals, and out-of-state investors had moved in. More fragile land was platted; Ocean Shores grew, with seaside motels, eateries, and a convention center; and razor clamming continued apace.

I visit Ocean Shores mostly to go to the area's lone supermarket and environmental interpretive center. I clam some miles up the coast, where forest reaches all the way down to the beach. My favorite access is near Connor Creek. I cross the creek and walk through pines and evergreen huckleberry, and then through marshy areas and dune grass to the shore. I've done this walk so many times I can picture it perfectly. Sometimes a few ducks swim in the brushy puddles; occasionally a hawk flies low, searching for prey. White flowers of dune strawberries dot the sandy path in season.

The motel I frequent is pretty much unchanged from the day it was built in the 1960s, just as Ocean Shores was launching: a one-story building with four studio units, constructed by the owner with his own hands out of plywood. The outdoor clam kitchen has eight

In the mid-1960s, model and coastal resident Teri Lee McDougal posed next to a wood razor clam sculpture, an icon of Ocean Shores. Not long thereafter the sculpture was stolen and never returned. An examination of the clam reveals that its foot and pointed toe face the wrong way. As seen in the photo of an actual clam, a clam's foot and toe face toward the hinge of the clam—that is, to the back. The anatomical error was never noticed or at least apparently never commented on during all the time the sculpture was in place. Courtesy Aberdeen Museum of History

shallow porcelain sinks built into a counter, four on each side, under a shed roof. It's tucked behind the storage building by alder trees and salmonberry. There's a hose and screened table for cleaning the sand off your clams, and cold water running at each sink station. People talk as they clean. "Where'd you clam?" "How'd you do?" It's hard work cleaning a limit, or a couple of limits, and chatting makes the chore go more easily. The cutting boards are worn, and the pot for boiling water to dip the clams is black from years over a propane flame. Little has changed in the twenty-five years I've been going. The same black pot, the same dented colander hung on the wall. These small working people's resorts used to be all over the razor clam beach areas, with generous clam kitchens laid out for the practical work of cleaning clams.

Now these places have mostly disappeared in favor of more conventional motels, and clam kitchens are often afterthoughts.

Long Beach and Ocean Shores are the two geographic poles and main tourist destinations of Washington's razor clamming beaches, which line the southern third of the state for fifty-three miles from the Columbia River north to Kalaloch. Washington is the epicenter of razor clamming on the West Coast because of the density of clams in these ocean beaches and their proximity to people. There are few razor clams in California, and just one main clamming beach in Oregon—Clatsop Beach, just south of the Columbia River. A good number of Oregonians come to Washington to razor clam.

Alaska has plenty of razor clams and razor clam habitat along its convoluted southern coastline, but this habitat is difficult to reach even by boat, and the human population is small. Razor clamming is popular but concentrated along the eastern shore of Cook Inlet, more than a three-hour drive from Anchorage. The number of recreational digging trips in a year is about what Washington gets on a couple of good weekends. In British Columbia, the best habitat is on Haida Gwaii, formerly known as the Queen Charlotte Islands, home to the Haida people. The archipelago is accessible only by plane or boat.

By contrast, Washington's razor clamming beaches are just minutes away from coastal cities and a few hours' drive from Seattle and other major population centers. You take the freeway, then smaller roads heading west, passing through evergreen forests and grasslands and small cities. The drive through these landscapes is a pleasure; plus, you remember the last time you dug, and the time a sheen of water turned the beach into a mirror and you walked on clouds, and that trip when the clams were so hard to find. So many trips, so many years. Finally you reach the coast, with its shore pines and dunes, and make the short hop to the ocean via the beach access

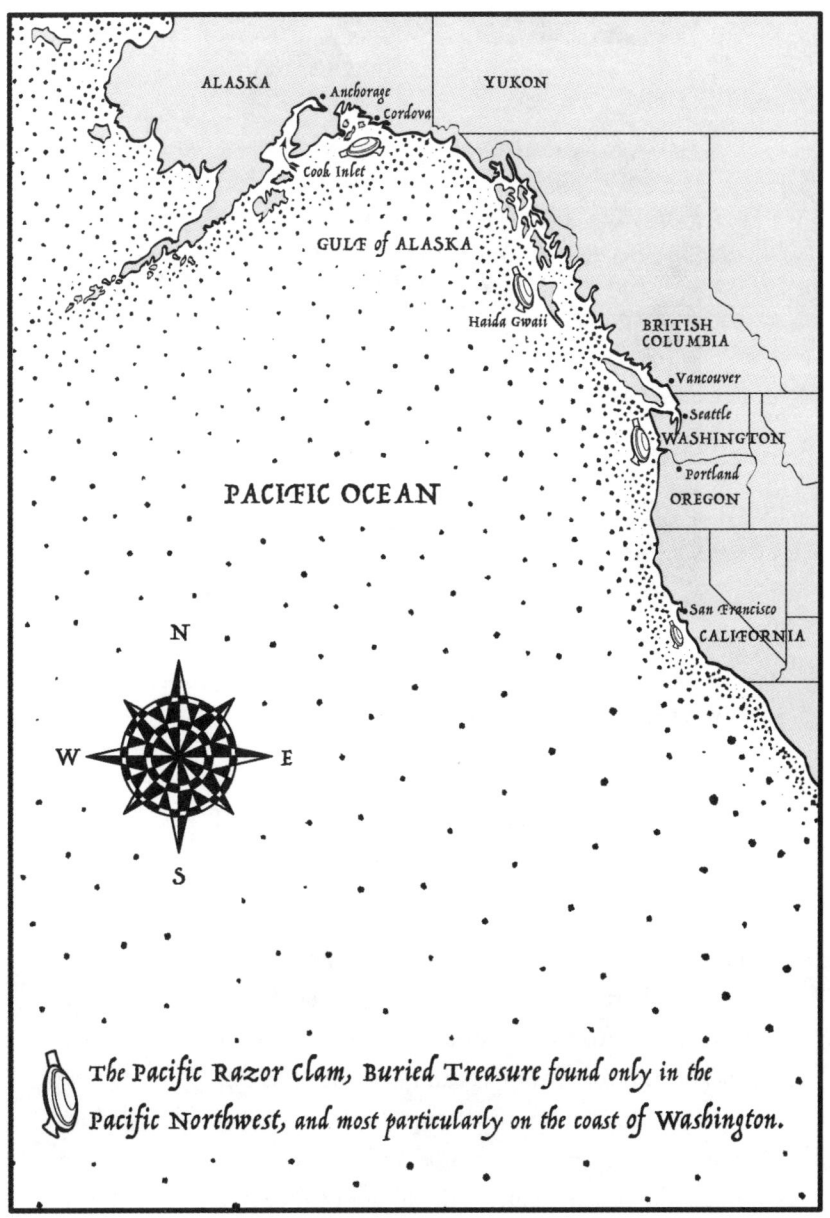

The Pacific razor clam is found only on the west coast of North America, especially from northern Oregon to Alaska. Map by Cynthia Hall

Marilyn Thomson with a beautifully polished wood razor clam trophy honoring her victory in the 2015 Long Beach Razor Clam Festival fritter-cooking contest. But in an oft-repeated error, the razor clam has its foot facing the wrong direction. Why is this error so common when people dig and clean thousands of razor clams every season? Perhaps it's the unconscious overlay of human organization onto the rest of the natural world—feet and toes are supposed to face front! Or maybe it's just the hurry everybody's in to get the clams onto the dinner table. Courtesy Laurie Anderson

roads. The car is more than a car when it drives over the scraped sand of these approaches. Yes, sometimes it's just fifty yards to the beach, but in that short stretch you traverse from civilization to wild ocean and open sky. And because it is so convenient, all ages and even handicapped razor clammers can make the journey.

You can drive for miles along the beach if you like, surf and sandpipers on one side, driftwood and dunes on the other. The state considers the beaches part of the highway system, though there are no lanes or markers. The speed limit is twenty-five miles per hour. Sometimes people get overexcited and drive in mad circles, "cutting doughnuts." Not officially permitted, of course.

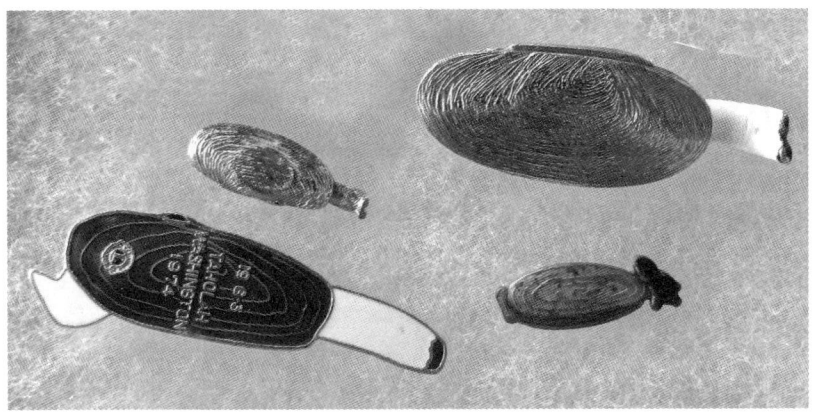

Examples of razor clam jewelry from the collection of the Museum of the North Beach. Lower left, the Taholah Lions Club pin gets the clam anatomy right—the toe is pointing toward the hinge side of the clam. Lower right, the small razor clam pin sports a fireman's hat. The two pins at top are ersatz gold. Big or small, razor clams are an icon of the Washington coast.

Beach driving has practical roots and dates from the days when coastal roads were few or nonexistent. Supplies and mail arrived by ship and then were motored along the beach to settlers and outposts. But the hard, moist sand of the upper beach quickly became a playground for car races and outings. The automobile and the beach were a happy match.

Attempts to curtail beach driving have been to little avail, though some summer and other special restrictions are in place. So you leave the city on the freeway, and your metal horse delivers you to the untamed ocean near Ocean Shores, or Long Beach, or some other location, and awaits to take you home when razor clamming is done. Very convenient. Being able to drive a car right onto the beach helps make razor clamming a lifetime activity. Neither age nor disability is necessarily a deterrent. And with a disability license, another person can even harvest for you. Stop razor clamming just because you have a herniated disc? No sirree. Folks tend to give up razor clamming under only two conditions: they have died or become vegetarian.

"CLAMILY FRITTERS"
2015 Long Beach Razor Clam Fritter Contest Winner
Makes 4 to 6 servings

A giant clam fritter, cooked in a fifteen-foot frying pan, was the highlight of the Long Beach Razor Clam Festival in the 1940s. The city restored its defunct festival in 2013, and the following year organizers brought back a version of the clam fritter event, this time as a competition between local culinary-arts high school students. Marilyn Thomson won the competition during its first year, and then again the second year with a revised version of her original recipe. The revised recipe takes advantage of cranberries as well as razor clams, thus combining two of the region's most famous ingredients.

Thomson is as much a baker as a cook, and her instructions for making the fritter batter include adding the eggs one at a time to the dry ingredients, as a baker might, and as her mother taught her.

FOR THE SWEET-AND-SPICY TARTAR SAUCE
- 1 cup mayonnaise
- ⅓ cup minced fresh cranberries
- 2 cloves garlic, minced
- 1½ teaspoon Cajun seasoning (or other "kick"—such as sriracha or chile pepper—to taste)
- ¼ teaspoon sweet paprika
- 1½ teaspoons fresh lemon juice
- ½ cup honey
- 2 tablespoons chopped fresh parsley

FOR THE FRITTERS
- 2 strips bacon, chopped
- ⅓ cup finely chopped onion
- 1 stalk celery, finely chopped

⅓ cup parboiled new potatoes (from about 3 potatoes, red or yellow)

3 cups panko bread crumbs, divided

1 cup all-purpose flour

1 tablespoon baking powder

1 teaspoon salt

½ teaspoon freshly ground black pepper

3 eggs, beaten

3 tablespoons whole milk

⅓ cup grated Parmesan cheese

1 to 1¼ cups minced razor clams

1 cup clam juice (reserved from cleaning; see note)

Oil, for frying

Lemon wedges, for serving

To make the sweet-and-spicy tartar sauce

In a medium-sized bowl, mix the mayonnaise, cranberries, garlic, Cajun seasoning, paprika, lemon juice, honey, and parsley. Set aside.

To make the fritters

In a large pan, sauté the chopped bacon over medium-high heat until cooked through. Remove the cooked bacon, leaving the fat in the pan, and sauté the onion and celery in the same pan. Grate the potatoes, discarding the skins (the potatoes should more or less crumble).

Put 2 cups of the panko into a small bowl. In a separate large bowl, combine the flour, remaining 1 cup of panko, baking powder, salt, and pepper. Add the eggs, one at a time, and whisk well. Add the milk, mix again, then add the Parmesan cheese, clams and clam juice, cooked onion and celery, grated potato, and bacon. Use your fingers to mix well (the batter will be thick), then form small patties by making a ball of the batter, dredging in panko and flattening, or push the dredged ball into a biscuit or cookie cutter, or into the bottom of a lightly oiled measuring cup. Touch up the finished patties with additional panko, if needed. Heat ¼ inch oil in a skillet or cast-iron pan over medium-high heat. Add a few patties to the pan (taking care not to overcrowd them), and fry until golden brown. Repeat with the remaining patties. Serve hot, accompanied with the tartar sauce and lemon wedges.

Note: Let the cleaned clams sit overnight in a bag in the refrigerator so that the clam juice will collect. If you don't have enough clam juice, supplement with water and a little salt to make one cup.

CHAPTER 3
SACRED TREATIES

THE Washington Department of Fish and Wildlife divides the state's razor clamming Arcadia into five management areas. The Long Beach area stretches twenty-four miles and is the largest section. Twin Harbors extends six miles; Copalis (which includes Ocean Shores), eleven miles; Mocrocks, seven miles; and Kalaloch, which is within Olympic National Park and the only beach without direct car access, five miles. Fifty-three miles in total. The management areas are separated by geographic features like bays and rivers, and they are managed by a variety of authorities, primarily the state but also tribal authorities and others. It's a lot of territory. All the beaches are wide and flat, and in places so uninterrupted along their lengths that the misty distances seem like the end of time itself. Bluffs and trees back some locations. Others have dunes and wetlands, or human structures. The beaches themselves are pretty similar. If it weren't for landmarks inland from them—a tall tree or the roof of a house—you'd hardly know where you were. Most people have their favorite spots near a particular outcropping or a certain creek dribbling into the ocean, or just near the beach access road. They return to these favored areas time and time again.

The beaches are in counties that traditionally have depended on natural resources like timber and fish. With those in eclipse since

Razor clams displayed with woven baskets on a Quinault Indian Nation beach. Razor clams and basketry are both integral parts of QIN culture. Courtesy Quinault Indian Nation and Larry Workman

the 1960s, and in decline even from the 1920s, cities like Aberdeen in Grays Harbor County and Long Beach in Pacific County have long suffered boom-and-bust cycles and social problems. Per capita income is lower than the state average, and unemployment is high. Populations are not much greater than they were a hundred years ago, and in fact are slowly shrinking. Many young people, like Nirvana musician Kurt Cobain, Aberdeen's most famous native son, leave as soon as they can.

Coastal tourism is critical for these counties, and local officials conjure monthly events to bring in people and dollars. Fireworks, classic-car shows, kite festivals, runs, beachcombers' fairs, and musical weekends are some of the regular offerings, plus the razor clam festivals and the state-organized razor clamming days. According to Randy Dennis, principal of a hardware and general merchandise chain, sales jump 25 percent on a clamming day, no matter the weather. If it's sunny, they sell sun hats. If it's raining, they sell slickers and boots. One denizen of the Ocean Shores area says of clamming

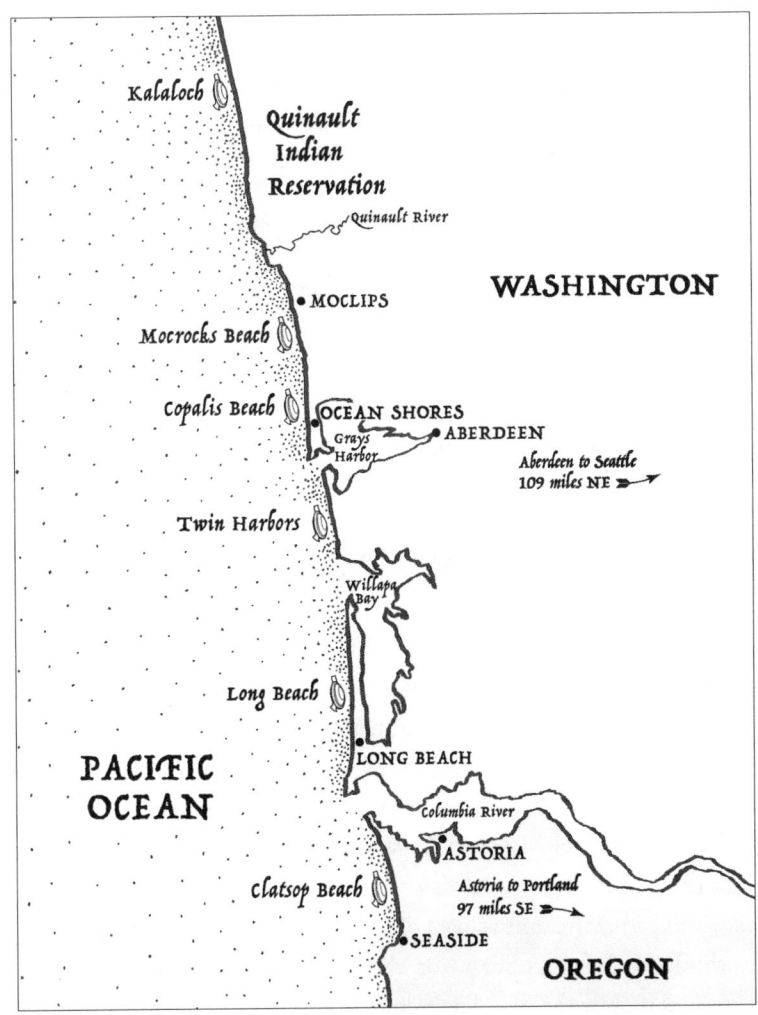

Razor clamming management areas of Washington and Oregon. Map by Cynthia Hall.

days, "I don't know the revenue but it's huge. Hotels are full, restaurants run out of food, gas stations pump dry. Cars are three deep on the beach. You almost need a parking permit, it's so crowded."

The Quinault Indian Nation (QIN), located on an isolated reservation thirty miles from Ocean Shores, has never had an iconic razor clam statue like Ocean Shores did and Long Beach does, but it does

SACRED TREATIES 43

have a fishing treaty: "our all-mighty sacred treaty with the United States," as one tribal fisherman put it. That treaty adds unique twists to Washington's razor clamming phenomenon.

The QIN numbers about three thousand tribal members, including people of Quinault, Queets, Quileute, Hoh, Chinook, Chehalis, and Cowlitz heritage, all of whose ancestors traditionally razor clammed in the highly productive beaches north and south of Ocean Shores. About half of the QIN people live on the reservation, and the rest mostly in neighboring areas. To reach the reservation, you drive the lone coastal road till it ends, heading north from Ocean Shores paralleling the ocean. The road enters the reservation and tribal village of Taholah by the Quinault River, then peters out into forest and dispersed human habitation occupying an area roughly one-quarter the size of Rhode Island. On or off the reservation, virtually every Quinault member has dug razor clams at some time. "Razor clams are part and parcel of tribal life, and a staple food for some," says Ed Johnstone, the QIN's policy spokesperson. "They're guaranteed to appear at festivals and Sunday dinners."

In 2013 QIN hosted that year's Canoe Journey, and tribal members dug and froze razor clams for many weeks in preparation. When they welcomed eighty-nine large canoes from seventy-five tribes, plus thousands of guests, after a paddle journey of hundreds of miles, they served razor clams as part of the celebration and feasting. It was unthinkable not to offer razor clams, along with other traditional foods, as part of the five-day event.

Every August there's a back-to-school dig for tribal families and kids. The dig takes place over two consecutive days, and participants gather on the tribe's reservation beach near Point Grenville. It's a chance to earn money for clothes, backpacks, and iPads in sunny summer weather. The tribe's commercial "buy truck" is right there to weigh out and pay cash for the clams.

For many years the Quinault people could razor clam only on the reservation beaches, and off reservation on public beaches with the

Canoe landing near keyhole rock on the Quinault Indian reservation in 2013, when the Quinault Indian Nation hosted the annual Canoe Journey event. Courtesy Quinault Indian Nation and Larry Workman

same recreational opportunities afforded to all state residents.

Two landmark court decisions transformed the situation and fishing for everyone in Washington. First came the so-called Boldt decision of 1974—the case of *United States v. Washington*—in which U.S. District Court judge George Hugo Boldt affirmed the right of Washington's tribes to fish for salmon "in common with all citizens" in their "usual and accustomed grounds and stations." That language was from the treaties of 1854 and 1855, concluded by Isaac Stevens, then superintendent of Indian Affairs and later governor, with more than twenty Indian tribes in what was then Washington Territory. The treaties ceded millions of acres in return for reservation lands and the ability to retain certain rights; terms were less negotiated than harshly forced on the tribes.

Boldt, a conservative appointed by President Dwight D. Eisenhower, was tasked with determining what the treaties meant for the modern era. He heard testimony from legal scholars, anthropologists, historians, and tribal elders, and then said that fishing "in common

SACRED TREATIES 45

with all citizens" meant the opportunity to harvest 50 percent of the allowable catch, plus the right to co-manage the resource.

The ruling created shock and controversy—half the salmon!—and, for its part, the state fought Boldt's interpretation all the way to the U.S. Supreme Court, which refused to consider the appeal in 1975.

In 1994, twenty years after Judge Boldt's landmark decision addressing salmon, U.S. District Court judge Edward Rafeedie presided over another protracted legal battle, a continuation of the original *U.S. v. Washington*, this time addressing shellfish rights. Rafeedie, appointed to the bench by President Ronald Reagan, listened to experts and spent a week touring shellfish beds and commercial operations by plane, van, and boat.

Judge Rafeedie, like Judge Boldt, interpreted the treaty language as the Indians would have understood it at the time. After hearing testimony that the "right of taking fish" in the 1850s would have meant harvesting anything that lived in the sea—not only fish but also clams, oysters, geoducks, crab, and marine mammals—Rafeedie delivered another shock to fishers and the general public by extending treaty fishing rights to include naturally occurring shellfish on privately owned lands.

The crucial treaty paragraph reads: "The right of taking fish, at all usual and accustomed grounds and stations, is further secured to said Indians in common with all citizens of the Territory, and of erecting temporary houses for the purpose of curing, together with the privilege of hunting, gathering roots and berries, and pasturing their horses on open and unclaimed lands: *Provided, however, that they shall not take shellfish from any beds staked or cultivated by citizens*" (emphasis added).

The "Shellfish Proviso" in the Stevens Treaties, prohibiting Indians from taking shellfish in staked or cultivated beds, reinforced the understanding that Native people had shellfish harvest rights. Why would there be a qualification if the shellfish harvest right wasn't there in the first place?

Rafeedie's decision was appealed by the State of Washington to the U.S. Supreme Court, which in 1999 refused to consider the request. Sharing the shellfish fifty-fifty was the law. The Rafeedie decision addressed the tidelands of Puget Sound, full of oysters and hard-shell steamer clams, but it plainly had implications for all of Washington's shellfish and treaty tribes, and thus for razor clams as well.

Shortly after the Rafeedie decision, a QIN biologist showed up at the Washington Department of Fish and Wildlife (WDFW) office in Montesano. He informed the razor clam managers that the QIN intended to harvest razor clams the following year on the public beaches. It was a difficult meeting. As word spread of the planned tribal harvest, there was grumbling from the public and some coastal sports clubs protested, but the state was done with legal fighting and Fish and Wildlife quickly got on with the business of figuring out how to divide up the clams.

Justine James, a QIN cultural resources specialist, remembers being astonished by the Rafeedie decision. He realized it meant razor clamming was back in a huge way—50 percent of the razor clams in the usual and accustomed places. Those traditional grounds amounted to twenty-three miles, or more than 40 percent of Washington's prime razor clam beaches, including the razor clam management areas of Copalis, Mocrocks, and Kalaloch—basically everywhere but Long Beach and Twin Harbors.

"These treaties mean something," says John Hollowed, a non-Indian legal and policy advisor who has worked for more than twenty-five years at the Northwest Indian Fisheries Commission, a consortium of twenty Washington State Indian tribes. "These are obligations and guarantees that the United States and therefore the states need to do. They are not something that disappears with time."

QIN divides its 50 percent share of the clams between ceremonial/subsistence use and commercial digs. Tribal authorities supervise the digs and provide enforcement. The ceremonial/subsistence digs put food on the table and serve a variety of cultural purposes. They are

Quinault Indian Nation diggers with surf sacks. Courtesy Quinault Indian Nation and Larry Workman

open to any Quinault tribal member with an identification card, and there is a hundred-clam limit per dig. The commercial digs put money into pockets, as individuals harvest and then sell clams to the QIN seafood enterprise, which processes and markets them. Participating in a commercial dig requires a permit issued at no cost by QIN authorities.

There are only so many good clamming tides in a month. Out of necessity, tribal and public recreational razor clam digs take place during the same good low-tide periods around the full and new moons, but on different days. The two digs are like ships passing in the night. There are practical reasons for separation, to keep count of the number of diggers and clams taken, but it's emblematic of a situation that is often misunderstood or invisible to the public. Many, if not most, recreational clam diggers are unaware that their weekend digs are often bracketed by tribal subsistence or commercial efforts. The anger that exploded following the Boldt and Rafeedie decisions has eased with time and generational changes, but some coastal residents are still surprised or resentful when they see a tribal dig in progress; it just feels wrong to them.

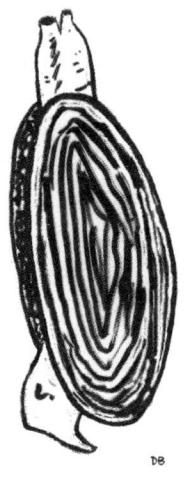

Few realize how the various tribal and state razor clam authorities have learned to cooperate to conserve and co-manage the resource, or that the QIN and other tribes have their own staff for fisheries management and enforcement. The tribes have a deep appreciation for the role razor clamming plays in the coastal economy, because they are part of it—business spikes at tribal enterprises like the Quinault Indian Casino and Resort, located near Ocean Shores, when there's a dig, just as it does for all businesses in the area. Razor clamming brings in people. "It's amazing how many people dig those fifteen clams for the recreational harvest. It blows your mind," says Johnstone, the QIN policy spokesperson.

I went clamming with tribal member Leon Frank on a subsistence/ceremonial dig in October. It was calm after days of wind-driven rain that had machine-gunned everyone right off the beach. More storms were on the way, but just now the slanting late-afternoon light was strong. The bellies of sandpipers flashed white as they swarmed by in tight formation just above the surf.

Only two people stood on the beach, Frank and myself. He was putting on hip-high boots and attaching a five-foot-long surf sack to his waist, just like the commercial diggers did in the early 1900s. It doesn't take long to dig a hundred clams, Frank assured me.

He was digging for his mom, he said. Going to bring her some clams. The tribal enterprise didn't have a market for the clams this month, he added with annoyance, so it was a subsistence dig, not a commercial one. Frank told me he could make two, three, four hundred bucks a tide on a commercial dig, easy. Five hundred to a thousand dollars on a good minus tide series. "That's enough for me for a month," he said in a singsong voice. "A way for me to survive. Pay my bills."

SACRED TREATIES   49

I realized just how important the commercial dig is to some Quinault people. Frank, fifty-one, was basically a professional digger, relying on the clams for a living. But there would be no commercial dig during this set of low tides.

"Is it hard to eat a hundred clams?" I asked.

He laughed. No, he said. Many households contain multiple families, and a hundred clams doesn't go that far. All this time the sun was descending, becoming a warm glow on the horizon, and he was pounding the beach with his shovel handle in a fan pattern, left to right—five hard pounds, a couple of steps, five more pounds, each bang throwing up a skirt of water and sand. But no clam shows. Normally they are all over, he said. He'd come early, way before the low tide while it was still light, to dig clams and not bother with a lantern. The water was thick with plankton, soupy in places like brown tea. Plenty of food for the clams. But the clams weren't showing despite all his pounding. When the clams are hiding like this there's not much you can do. It's just one of those things. Humans don't dominate the situation.

The breakers were coming in hard and rolling far up the shore; it made it difficult to cover much beach. Finally a hole appeared and Frank inserted the shovel, pulled back and compressed the sand, and reached in for the clam. The clams were starting to show now, and he was in constant motion, flowing and quick, just like the flocks of sandpipers and the light breeze.

"If I don't get them in one dig I move on," he said, thumping the beach with the shovel. I was seagulling him, you could say, although I wasn't clamming. Seagulling, Frank explained, was when somebody spotted you doing well and crowded in. Very impolite. Even on the populous state recreational digs, digging groups know to keep their distance from one another.

Nobody was seagulling on this beach. There were way more actual seagulls than people. I'd never been on a dig when the beach was so empty. There was literally no competition for the clams. As it became

Tribal digger Leon Frank "prospecting" for clams by banging the beach with the shovel handle, trying to force a show

dark and closer to low tide, a lantern light finally appeared far down the beach, near the tall, boxy shadow in the dunes that was the tribe's casino and resort. One other tribal digging party. A Quinault enforcement officer rolled by in a truck and waved. A small band of geese flew overhead, turning inland for the night. The rhythms here at the coast are nature's, but Frank at the moment was much too involved in stomping the beach like Rumpelstiltskin, splattering water and plankton soup like a kid in a puddle, to notice the geese or the last bit of light disappearing. He was just pounding the beach, intently scanning, bent over with eyes close to the beach on account of the darkness. His sack dragged behind him like a lizard's tail. He told me, and it was later confirmed, that he was one of best commercial diggers. I could well believe it, given his single-minded focus. The clams were showing now, and he gathered them with spare movements and swung his arm between his legs, launching the clams into the sack without rising from a crouch. He was aggressive and fast even though the day was slowing down and sliding to darkness. He'd bring about thirty-five clams to his mom, who perhaps was waiting at home, *ta'aWshi xa' iits'os*—in the traditional Quinault language, "hungry for clams."

Tribal cultures have formalized their thanks to salmon, in the salmon homecoming celebrations that honor the return of the fish in the fall, but according to Justine James, the QIN cultural resources specialist, there is no analog for razor clams, even though they've been a traditional food from time immemorial. James thought maybe some elders said a prayer before they went out, and typically some clams would be given to elders or contributed to a family meal. Frank expressed his appreciation in his own way. "A million clams last year for the tribe, a million for the state," he said, referring to the tribal and non-tribal harvest on Copalis and Mocrocks beaches. "That's amazing. And they tell us it's going to be as good this year. You dig, and then next month, and next year, you can come back to the same spot, and they keep showing up. Just go back to the same spot and get clams," he said in a voice tinged with wonder.

CLAMS WITH SNAP PEAS IN CHAMPAGNE VINAIGRETTE
Makes 4 servings

Briefly poaching razor clams in water produces clam meat that can be used in any number of ways. As ever, don't overcook, or the clams can become rubbery. Essentially, you're shocking the clams. Ed Johnstone, the QIN policy spokesperson, likes to eat barely poached razor clams with drawn butter. "Yum, yum," he says.

This recipe mixes the shocked clam meat with a champagne vinaigrette. Champagne vinegar is milder than other vinegars and a good match with the razor clams. Other vinegars can be too harsh.

- 1 tablespoon champagne vinegar
- 2 tablespoons olive oil
- 1 small clove garlic, pressed
- ¼ teaspoon dried thyme
- 1 tablespoon high-heat vegetable oil
- 30 snap peas, strings removed, chopped into thirds
- ¼ cup water
- ¼ teaspoon salt
- 2 cups razor clams, necks and diggers separated, from about 8 clams
- 3 tablespoons chopped parsley
- Freshly ground black pepper

In a small bowl, mix or whisk the vinegar, olive oil, garlic, and thyme. Set this dressing aside.

Have ready a large bowl of ice water to put the clams in when they finish cooking. In a large pan, heat the oil over high heat, then add the snap peas and stir-fry until blistered in spots, about 2 minutes. Remove the snap peas to a bowl. In a medium-sized pan, bring the water to a simmer, and add the salt. Add the diggers, stir, and cover the pan. After 15 to 30 seconds add the necks, stir, cover, and cook about 15 seconds to a minute more, until just starting to firm (the cooking time depends on the size of the clams—don't overcook!). Remove the clams to the bowl of ice water to stop the cooking. Reserve the cooking liquid.

Drain the clams and chop them on the diagonal. Add them to the snap peas, along with dressing to taste and a splash of the cooking liquid. Add half of the parsley and salt and pepper to taste. Mix well. Garnish with the remaining parsley. Serve at room temperature or chilled.

CHAPTER 4

ECOLOGY AND ANATOMY

At first glance, Washington's sandy beaches look empty of life. A few sturdy seagulls and shape-shifting flocks of sandpipers only emphasize the emptiness. Just sand and sky as far as the eye can see. Around the world, such beaches are not especially biologically productive, lacking hard substrates like rock on which life can anchor itself or find shelter. But Washington's beaches are, in fact, just the opposite: stupendously productive. A great city of razor clams, a megalopolis, thrives hidden in the sand.

The nearshore waters are crowded and fecund as well. When biologist Harvey McMillin dragged his net through the surf in the 1920s and looked through a microscope, he found the water full of phytoplankton. These tiny single-celled algae were the razor clams' food. Specifically, he found diatoms, a kind of phytoplankton with cell walls made of silica. The plethora helped account for the abundance of razor clams, he wrote, adding that the surf diatoms often accumulated or formed colonies in such numbers that they colored the water brown or greenish and washed ashore in layers that looked like mud.

It's the same today. It's hard to believe the green and brown deposits darkening the pristine sand are not an oil spill or scummy pollution, but are in fact the clams' nourishment. The razor clams extend their siphon from the depths to the surface like a straw, ingesting

Razor clams were bigger in the old days, as this postcard reveals. Courtesy Museum of the North Beach

food through one tube and expelling waste through the other. Nearly every day is a Thanksgiving feast.

In the 1970s, three researchers went to Copalis Beach, the very beach where I wrested my first clam from the sand, to study the phytoplankton. Joyce Lewin, Charles Schaefer, and Donald Winter found that diatoms were not only abundant more or less permanently but also were actually most plentiful in winter. That surprised them; phytoplankton are supposed to teem in summer, when light abounds, and to reduce or even disappear in winter, due to the lack of light and warmth. But the surf diatoms were proliferating in winter as well as in summer.

Intrigued by the "extraordinary abundance of surf diatoms and their anomalous seasonal variations," the trio spent more than a decade investigating Washington's razor clam surf-zone ecology. Productive razor clam beaches had distinctive features, they noted: the beaches were long, wide, and extraordinarily flat, with slopes of just one to three degrees. Breakers created a dynamic high-energy environment. The offshore areas were as flat or even flatter than the beaches themselves. All this tabletop created an immense expanse of shallow water in which the surf diatoms thrived by way of tricks that would do a Las Vegas magician proud.

First, the surf diatoms went on a vertical migration, a number rising up to the surface from the sand before dawn and sinking back down before sunset. Then, as if this daily levitation were not enough, at the surface the diatoms attached themselves to and stabilized the foamy bubbles created by wave action and turbulence, thus further enabling them to stay at the top of the water column and utilize the sun's energy via photosynthesis.

No one quite understands how they manage these tasks, rising up and merging with bubbles, and staying close to the sun. Diatoms are diverse, successful, and mysterious organisms, reluctant to reveal their tricks. At any rate, once diatoms are at the surface, waves—and in winter the strong seasonal winds and storms—push them toward the shore, where they continue to photosynthesize even if deposited on the beach. Storms stir up the bottom and extend the surf zone to as much as half a mile, according to the researchers. Within this surf zone the diatoms are in regular circulation, moving from the beach to the far side of the breakers and back again in a merry-go-round of riptides, gyres, wind, and waves. This stirring up accounts for the greater numbers of diatoms in winter, the researchers said.

Reading their paper, I remembered the chaotic waves that knocked me over during the Long Beach Razor Clam Festival. The ocean water had been a weird frothy brown, the color of peat moss. I thought it looked cursed. Even the foam of breaking waves was dark instead of cloud white. In hindsight, the murk must have been the diatoms enjoying ideal conditions from an expanded surf zone, with turbulence and onshore wind pushing them into reproductive and photosynthetic overdrive. Not at all what I thought was going on.

Lewin, Schaefer, and Winter found that beach structure went a long way toward explaining why Washington's beaches had huge numbers of diatoms feeding razor clams, while other nearby beaches, like those south of Clatsop Beach in Oregon, had fewer or none.

Those beaches were not quite so long or wide or flat, or had different sand grain sizes or amounts of certain minerals. Such variations corresponded neatly with reduced or absent surf diatoms.

You might think that phytoplankton would run out of nutrients on long, flat beaches with high-energy surf zones, since they maintain huge populations and reproduce at high rates. But they don't. Runoff from land—all that rain that so discouraged Lewis and Clark when they wintered on the coast—as well as deep ocean upwellings help replenish nutrients.

The researchers discovered something else as well: after digesting the diatoms the razor clams secreted waste back into the ecosystem as ammonium, a form of nitrogen. Nitrogen is a critical nutrient for phytoplankton growth and often the limiting factor. So razor clams eat the phytoplankton, then recycle the nitrogen waste back so the phytoplankton can prosper, just like human farmers might return manure to the fields to fertilize and grow crops. What a system.

Now, every time I go razor clamming, I think about these two pragmatists, the razor clams and the diatoms, living together hand in glove. If Long Beach were to truly recognize the prodigious events taking place a stone throw's away at the beach, it would have to add a surf diatom to its collection of giant charms, I realized.

And not just any surf diatom, but a specific one: *Attheya armatus*. This is the surf diatom that predominates. Under a microscope it has a square body and filament-like "legs," actually hard structures called horns (*armatus* is Latin for "horn").

Curiously enough, the dominant diatom species has shifted several times over the decades. Data is pretty good, because razor clams have long been an important food item and hence their environment an object of attention. When McMillin examined Washington's surf plankton community in the 1920s, he primarily found *Aulacodiscus kittonii*, a surf diatom that looks like a sand dollar. But by the 1940s that surf diatom had disappeared, replaced by the star-shaped *Asterionella socialis*, probably due to the completion of the first major dam

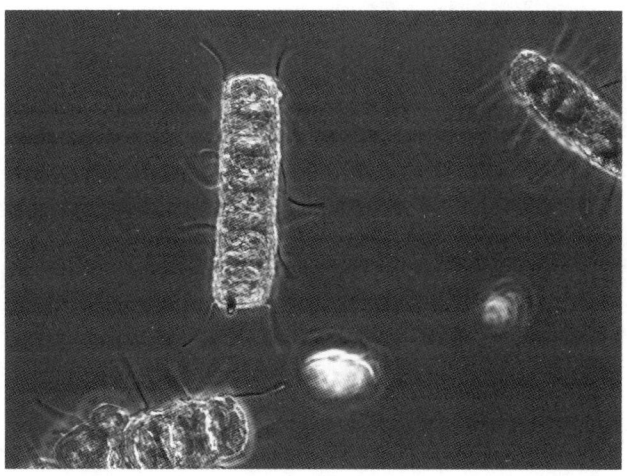

The microscopic diatom *Attheya armatus*, the razor clam's primary food. Though a single-celled organism, *Attheya armatus* often links up to form chains of five or more, or even several hundred. The short chain pictured here, resembling a caterpillar, is roughly 20 to 25 percent the length of a grain of sand. Courtesy WDFW and Zachary Forster

on the Columbia River in 1937, which altered the volume, timing, and character of the river's sediment discharge into the Pacific Ocean.

In the 1950s, *Attheya armatus* pushed aside the star-shaped *Asterionella socialis*, and Washington's razor clams have dined on that surf diatom ever since. *Attheya armatus*, at one time named *Chaetoceros armatum*, hadn't been recorded before on the West Coast. *Attheya*'s ascension to top dog did not coincide with any obvious changes or human actions. Researchers believe that it's an invasive species, or, to put it less pejoratively, a highly adaptable non-native species. Possibly it hailed from New Zealand, which also has flat, sandy beaches and large surf diatom densities. Wherever it came from, the diatom, very large in size, thrived on Washington's coast. The change in species didn't appear to bother the razor clams. Nearly every day was still Thanksgiving.

Razor clams eating these surf diatoms grow from fragile nothings to three inches, what the biologists call recruit size, in about a year, and top out with shells about 6.25 inches in length. Up in Alaska, where the waters are colder and more protected and growth is more seasonal, the clams develop more slowly, grow a little longer in length, and can live twice as long, or more, as the six or so years likely for Washington's clams, although the latter might live a few years longer if they weren't harvested so regularly.

Mature clams generally spawn in the spring or early summer in the Pacific Northwest, and as late as August in Alaska's cooler waters. Razor clams are born either male or female and stay that way their entire life—not a given with marine creatures, which sometimes casually flip-flop between sexes. Ripe razor clam females broadcast eggs into the water, and the males sperm. Once the action gets going it triggers an orgy, and in calm weather a foamy white slick can develop at the tideline. The egg and sperm meet up and the fertilized eggs develop into a gazillion larval clams, which to some extent are moved by currents and winds, but mostly stay near the bottom and close to home. After about ten weeks they wash ashore on the beaches, tiny versions of their adult selves. Ocean conditions and the vagaries of tides, currents, storms, and predators like jellyfish and filter-feeding fish determine how the clams fare and where and whether they make land. Overall, only a fraction survive. Eventually, the juveniles are strong enough to dig in with their foot and stay anchored just below the surface on the beach, though they are still not safe. Crabs and birds eat them. Surf or cars can crush them, and storms can upend the beach and wash them right out of the sand.

You are less inclined to ponder life cycles and razor clam anatomy when you have a full limit to clean and breakfast is waiting. But I never fail to be entranced by the puzzle of siphons, tubes, digger, and internal organs, and so I met with David Cowles, professor of marine biology, to dissect a razor clam. We rendezvoused at the University of

Walla Walla's summer facility on Puget Sound amid evergreen trees and the heady fragrance of clean salt water. Cowles had grown up in the city of Forks on the Olympic Peninsula. He said his dad hadn't been educated but loved nature, and they took long walks together in the woods and along the beach to look at things, and that was how he came to study science and the natural world.

We started with the smooth, shiny razor clam shell. Two valves, lateral plates of calcium carbonate, make up the shell, he pointed out. A bivalve.

"Wait a minute," I said. "A bivalve has nothing to do having two siphons, an in and an out?"

"No, it's a term for the two components that make up the shell, attached by a hinge."

Somehow I'd always assumed that the word *bivalve* referred to the intake and outflow of the organism, presumably controlled by a couple of valves. But that was dead wrong. Those little hard-shell clams at the bottom of my seafood stew were bivalves because they had two hard plates—two valves—hinged together to make a shell. No other reason. Biologists use the term *valve* in a special way, I realized, and that is how they sidestep the conundrum of having to say the clam has two shells that make up the shell. Two valves make up the shell.

The confusion of valves cleared up, we turned our attention to the translucent peel that covers the shell. In most species of clam, this covering—the periostracum (*peri* is Latin for "around," *ostracum* for "shell")—wears off, but in razor clams it lasts a lifetime, a glossy garment that gives the clam its golden brown color and facilitates gliding.

There is a brain, Cowles told me, but it's not much more than some pairs of nerve ganglia located near the top of the foot, almost microscopic. Since the brain center, or head, determines the top of an organism, what we think of as the bottom of the clam is actually the top, or anterior. The neck or siphon—the part sometimes sticking up from the sand—is the bottom, or posterior.

But while the clams from an anatomical perspective may be in the beach upside down, their heads literally in the sand, they are not stupid or unaware. Despite a tiny brain, they sense light and vibration, and they have the capability of orientation—all the clams positioning themselves in the beach exactly the same way, hinges toward the sea. This haunts my imagination. Millions of clams, not in the sand randomly, but lined up as orderly as soldiers on parade, their hinges and thick part of their shells facing the surf.

Clams also have a heart, which somehow surprised me. It's embedded in the visceral sac and hard to pick out. Cowles said razor clams have an open circulatory system with a short aorta that ends, the clear blood diffusing through the organism. It is like oil in a car; there's a pump, but the motor oil simply drips through the engine.

Razor clam blood is copper-based, not iron-based like human blood, and the copper compound gives the blood a bluish tinge. The blood supplies oxygen and nutrients, and also serves as pneumatic fluid that, directed by muscles, gives the clam a hydrostatic skeleton. With this mechanism, the clam's foot can twist, swell, pulse, and burrow with the rambunctious agility of two kids rolling about in a sheet and the strength of a weightlifter.

As we proceeded with the dissection, I realized that the razor clam is a master of double and triple uses. The dark gills not only absorb oxygen from seawater, like lungs, but also filter out the plankton food using a sophisticated network of tiny channels and filaments.

Anybody who has seen razor clams knows about the two tubes in the neck, one to ingest food and the other to eliminate waste. When you clean razors, the two channels are as plain as the piping to and from your hot water tank. But the ingesting inhalant tube also does double duty as the channel for expulsion of pseudofeces, a mixture of water and sand. That's the spurting you see at the beach that sometimes accompanies feeding and burrowing, and the spurt reenacted by the Long Beach razor clam sculpture on the hour. Actual digestive waste is disposed of via the smaller exhalant siphon, the

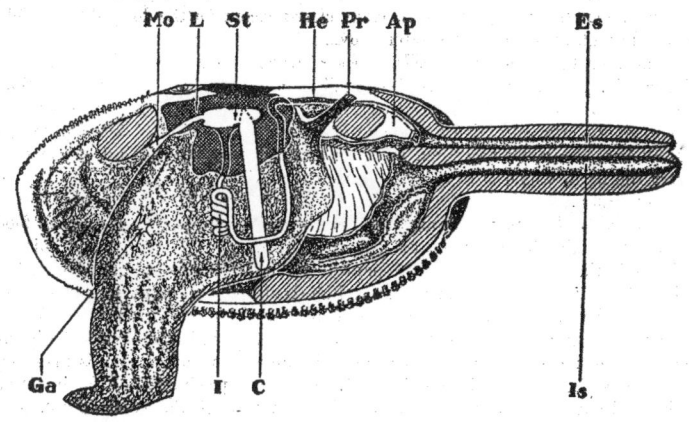

Anatomical drawing from a 1925 report on razor clam growth and maturity by three noted authorities of the time, F. W. Weymouth, H. C. McMillin, and H. B. Holmes. C is the crystalline style, Es the exhalant siphon, Is the inhalant siphon, and He the heart. Others: Ap, anal papilla; Ga, pedal ganglion; I intestine; L, liver; Mo, mouth; Pr, posterior retractor; St, stomach. Bureau of Fisheries, Government Printing Office

one always closest to the sea. The two tubes of the siphon are united as one neck-like continuation from the mantle, the thin sheet that envelops the clam's body and grows the shell. It's entirely obvious on inspection but nevertheless surprising that the siphon is an extension of the mantle, like the neck of a turtleneck sweater. Microscopic cilia within the mantle and siphons, hair-like projections that "lash sharply in one direction and return slowly . . . like a myriad of tiny oars," keep water steadily flowing in and out of the clam's siphons and through the organism.

The oddity that most people experience every time they clean a clam is a gelatinous rod that pops out of the clam's innards like a jack-in-the-box. This transparent "crystalline style" sits in a sac and extends into the stomach; turned by cilia, it rotates against the gastric shield, abrading digestive enzymes. Whenever I hear someone cleaning a razor clam gasp, "What the heck is that?" I'm pretty sure the crystalline style has shot out of the clam. The style is generally an inch or two in length, unattached to anything, a geometric rod that looks completely out of place. Researchers are as startled as clam diggers to encounter the crystalline style, because it is an unusual structure and possibly the only example of a fully rotating part in the animal kingdom.

Is the Pacific razor the fastest-digging clam in the world? *Siliqua patula* is certainly fast and good at disappearing if you aren't quick about your business. Most other bivalves just sit there in their shell castles, happily buried in mud and gravel or confident and brazenly exposed like an oyster. The Pacific razor has chosen a different survival path: streamlined speed. "The distinctive characteristic of the razor clam is its mobility," wrote the biologist McMillin in 1924. Razor clams live in a dynamic environment. In summer, tides and currents build berms and bars. In winter, storms scour, flatten, and reshape the sand. The surf is often pounding. But by using its clever foot and beach smarts, razor clams adapt and prosper.

The razor clam's speed isn't only in its foot, it must be admitted. As soon as the clam recognizes danger, *whoosh*, it contracts its neck. Sometimes you can see the neck disappearing down a hole like a fat white worm. The clam then wastes no time employing its powerful foot to "dig to China."

Though pounding the beach to make the clams show is an effective harvesting strategy, often it's better if you can sneak up on the clams and catch them while they're feeding, the siphon flush with the beach or sticking up—that is, "necking," or, as some have called it, "snouting." When necking, the clam creates a *V*-shaped ripple as the water retreats. Diggers keep a sharp eye out for such telltales. A letter sent by a man to the Washington Department of Fish and Wildlife described his "17-year-old high school drop-out self" trying to make a few bucks in 1930 at the beginning of the Depression. He had gotten a commercial clamming license but was doing poorly till a barefoot Native woman showed him a different way of doing things. She stood still as the water came in and swirled around her feet, and,

Razor clams sometimes don't show for reasons no one can fathom. Twin Harbors is especially notorious for occasionally fickle clams. Bob McCausland was a well-known cartoonist and illustrator at the *Seattle Post-Intelligencer* for thirty-three years before he retired to the Washington coast, where he continued penning cartoons including of razor clamming. Bob McCausland cartoon, courtesy Ruth McCausland

as the wave receded, looked intently to spot a *V*-shaped ripple or protruding siphon. Then she thrust her shovel blade into the sand behind the show on the seaward side to get the clam. "'No pound beach!' she exclaimed. 'No good pound beach!'"

The man continued, "I sort of followed the old lady around watching her, and when she peered down at the sand as the waves were running out I did too. I finally saw the little dimple the feeding clams left with their siphon. I dug like she did and began getting clams, two or three with every outgoing wave. Soon the bag I trailed between my legs from a belt began getting heavy and hard to drag across the sand."

It was a lesson in observation and technique he never forgot, and, sixty-five years later, when he typed out his razor clamming recollections, the memory was still vivid. He later received his high school diploma in the army and then went to university, majoring in biology. Perhaps he was intrigued by razor clam behavior. They tend to intrigue that way. You just want to know more.

It's pretty intuitive how the clam manages to dig down in the sand: It extends its digger, inserts its hard, pointed toe, and flares the bottom of its foot all around to make an anchor. Then it uses strong retractor muscles to pull its streamlined shell down to that fixed point. Extend, anchor, pull. When pushing its digger into the sand the clam can also expand its shell, thus forming a base to leverage against, like a rock climber in a chimney pushing outward with both arms while reaching with a leg. The clam's speed is always reported as fast, with the more academic citing McMillin's hundred-year-old research. He investigated by attaching a string to the clam's neck using a bent pin hooked into the tough neck tissue between the two siphons. Not high-tech, but effective.

McMillin noted that sand is typically wetter and softer below the surface, and that in that locale the clams traveled quite rapidly, descending on average nine inches a minute, for short periods. That rate was a little higher than typical, he thought, but "possible where the sand is wet and the clam is in a hurry." He used clams still embedded in the sand for his investigations, because once the clam was removed, the hydraulic connection of sand, water, and clam was broken, and the clams often were slow to reestablish themselves and did not dig deep.

It wasn't the intention of Amos Winter and Anette Hosoi to overthrow the Pacific razor clam's reputation as a fast clam when they began their research in 2006. The MIT scientists wanted to develop a low-energy mechanical device for digging into the seafloor and anchoring human equipment, such as a research submersible or undersea cable. They looked at all manner of burrowing creatures for inspiration, settling on bivalves—and specifically the Atlantic razor clam, *Ensis directus*, whose burrowing ability was highly efficient. They developed a device mimicking its actions, called it the "RoboClam," and reaped a whirlwind of publicity.

According to these researchers, *Ensis directus* can dig about one centimeter a second, or twenty-four inches a minute. More than twice as fast as the Pacific razor clam. But then, they were measuring the clam in little glass beads in the laboratory, and it's hard to know if clams can keep up that speed for more than the shortest of distances. I'm a little suspicious of the historical in situ measurements as well, because *Ensis directus* lives in soft mud. If you look at online videos, you see people plucking these skinny clams from the beach as easily as pulling out a pencil. That would never happen with a streetwise *Siliqua patula* anchored in the sand. Furthermore, *Ensis directus* has been described as a small, weak creature with a squishy body. Hmm, *Siliqua patula* is more like Charles Atlas. So I'm not giving up on our local heroes. Still, *Ensis directus* digs fast, and East Coasters call them the Ferraris of the mollusk world. They can also jet in the water short distances, like a squid (which is also a mollusk), a handy trick.

Biologists have known for some time that many clams, including razor clams, forcibly close their shells to expel water and thus soften the sand below them for easier descent. The MIT researchers made an additional observation about the Atlantic razor clam's technique: when digging down, the clam contracted its shell in such a precise manner as to create a brief episode of quicksand around itself. Timing was everything. If the clam were to move its shell too slowly, the sand particles would collapse around the animal and not fluidize. But if the clam moved too quickly, it wouldn't give enough time for the sand particles and water to mix. When done just right, the clam made its way through something that more resembled water than solid sand, thus increasing speed and decreasing the energy required to descend.

Do Pacific razor clams perform the same legerdemain of localized fluidization, fluttering in the sand? Possibly, or perhaps they perform some similar sequence. They doubtless have a fine appreciation for the interactions of force, water, and sand particles. And but for an accident of fate, it could have been *Siliqua patula* fussed over and gracing the pages of the *LA Times*, the *Economist*, and *Scientific American*. Unfortunately, the Pacific razor clam does not receive much scientific attention. The specifics of Pacific razor clam burrowing are no doubt intricate, but they have little bearing on human health or resource management, and so are unlikely to be given a funded study.

Of course, anybody who has been to the beach and pressed damp sand with toes and then released them knows about changing resistance through pressure. And clammers quickly figure out that wiggling fingers loosens the sometimes concrete-dense sand around a clam and makes it easier to surround and grasp the quarry.

But another question haunted me, besides how the clam dug down. After the razor clam lowered itself two feet or deeper, using its powerful foot and retractor muscles, how did it dig itself back up? There was no point above the clam toward which to pull. There was no foot to extend upward and anchor in. So, how did the clam ascend? The stories celebrating the clam's speed didn't bother with this question, only with the downward sprint. Clams come up close to the surface all the time to feed, so it is a common-enough affair. But how?

I pondered this question while driving. I pondered it at night while lying in bed. I imagined myself a clam with a single foot. How would I move upward? There really seemed only one possible mechanism. The clam—with that clever leg, as mobile as an elephant's trunk and layered with longitudinal, circular, and tangential muscles—curled up, dug in, and became an anchor, and then hydraulically pushed against that fixed point. It became a living ratchet and thus inched its way upward. I guessed it might not inch its way up very quickly, but then it wasn't a safety mechanism like digging down to escape the pincers of a crab or teeth of a perch. The razor clam is a thoroughbred only when fleeing. The rest of the time it is a ruminant, strolling to the plankton pastures. To press against the sand and move upward, the sand would have to be firm, or perhaps the foot would expand like a camel's footpad, both of which seemed entirely plausible. Maybe the siphon could

A clam just removed from the sand, its foot still expanded all around to serve as an anchor

exhale some softening water into the sand above for the upward journey? Or maybe it would wait for just the right sand/water conditions? The literature is silent on the finer points of this upward locomotion.

However it all works, the razor clam is right at home in the sand. To see a clam dive back into its beach home is a memorable sight. Not long ago, I was clamming just after New Year's Eve. The weather was mild, and the low tide was just before dusk. I laid my net on the beach and counted in the diminishing wintry light. Fifteen, a full limit. As I stood, one medium-sized clam slipped out of the net. He was a frisky fellow and he immediately stretched his foot out from the shell and pointed it this way and that, and dug around. In a few seconds, he had worked the tip of his foot into the sand. Then, to my amazement, he poinged himself upright. His shell was as straight and vertical as a sapling. Of course, he wasn't done. In a matter of a few moments he slipped himself into the sand and disappeared. With each downward effort came a spurting slurry of sand and seawater out of the inhalant siphon. As it happened, whether by accident or because this was a smart little clam, he was correctly oriented with his hinge facing the ocean. He disappeared like a knife into a sheath in well under a minute. He was still digging, even though he was gone from sight, as I could tell from the disturbance on the surface from expelled water. Then a ripple of wave washed over, eliminating all trace of this epic, and he was gone.

ECOLOGY AND ANATOMY 69

Try as I might, I could never get this precise behavior to repeat. I've laid out mature clams and juveniles, hoping to watch an encore performance. Nope. I've helped the clams along by putting them in different locations, soft sand and hard, even digging and softening sand for them. No dice. I've seen clams dig themselves sideways into the beach, as if sliding into home plate, and then stop, apparently tuckered out. But never again this full swan dive into the sand. I would like to see this behavior again, but sometimes things happen only once in a lifetime.

SILVEY FAMILY FRIED RAZOR CLAMS
Makes 2 servings

Mike and Bebe Silvey were high-school sweethearts in the coastal city of Aberdeen, Washington, and they both razor clammed at the beaches a short drive away. They were in the same biology class, where Bebe made a poster about the razor clam life cycle. They are now long married and retired and live in Southern California, but they and their clan get together every year on the Washington coast for a razor clamming reunion.

Over the decades, Mike and his son Greg have evolved their recipe for frying clams. Their current preferred version features Asian-influenced ingredients, including tempura flour, Japanese panko, and coconut oil. Panko is a coarse-textured bread crumb that gives a clean taste and deep-fried crunch without actual deep frying, and is the go-to coating for many. Coconut oil adds a rich mouthfeel.

There are, of course, many recipes and variations for fried razor clams. Some dredge the clams, then dip in egg, and fry with the egg on the outside. Seasoned flours can be made in innumerable permutations. Some old-school recipes call for Ritz Cracker crumbs and baking at a high heat in lieu of frying.

Mike takes pride in digging fifteen clams with no broken shells, and equal pride in butterflying the clams expertly while cleaning, leaving the neck and digger attached to each other. It's a nice presentation at the table and testament to his skill. It's tricky to do because the neck and digger are barely attached once the clam is cleaned, and it has to be done precisely. Greg is less concerned with presentation and separates the digger and neck for better control while cooking. The digger is meaty and may take more cooking time, while the neck can turn rubbery in a matter of seconds. But some would scoff at anything but perfectly butterflied, completely intact clams on the plate. It's a debate Mike and his family have before every meal.

2 eggs

1 cup panko bread crumbs

1 cup tempura flour, seasoned with salt and freshly ground black pepper

7 razor clams, butterflied, whole or with diggers and necks separate

Coconut oil, as needed, for frying

In a medium bowl, beat the eggs with about ½ cup water (the mixture should be watery, not eggy). Place the panko and tempura flour into separate bags or on plates. Dredge the clams a few at a time in the flour (shake in the bag or roll on the plate), dip in the egg wash, shake or roll in the panko, and set on a tray. Repeat with the remaining clams.

In a cast-iron pan, heat ¼ inch coconut oil over medium hot. When the oil is hot enough to set the clams sizzling when you drop them in, but not so hot that the panko burns, add the clams a few at a time and cook for 30 seconds to a minute on each side, until just lightly golden. If desired, cook the meaty diggers separately from the necks. Change the oil if it starts to unduly darken or has too many burned crumbs.

The Silveys cook outside on the side burner of a gas grill or on a camp stove because of the mess. If increasing the recipe, keep the finished clams warm in a low oven as you cook the remaining batches, or serve at room temperature.

Note: Clams can vary markedly in size, so the amount of flour and other ingredients will vary as well.

KAREN'S FRY MIX
Makes about 3 cups, enough for 12 to 18 fried razor clams

Karen developed this mixture over several years. She dusts the razor clams with it, then fries them up in butter or a mixture of butter and oil. The fry mix is equally good on fish or pork chops. Since it requires various ingredients, it's best to mix up a good batch and keep it in the cupboard as a staple; it will keep three months or longer. The salt and spicing amounts are modest, allowing the mixture to be further customized for each application, or for the food to be salted after it's cooked, if desired.

1 cup all-purpose flour
½ cup white rice flour
1½ cup fine to medium-grind cornmeal
2 tablespoons sweet paprika
1¼ teaspoons garlic powder
2 teaspoons dried parsley
½ teaspoon onion powder
1 tablespoon cornstarch
1½ teaspoons salt
½ teaspoon cayenne
Freshly ground black pepper

Mix all ingredients to taste and store in a tightly covered jar.

CHAPTER 5

PAST ABUNDANCES

Eating razor clams has defined something essential in the Pacific Northwest for a long time. Every era has exploited the cornucopia in its own way. The Native coastal tribes ate the clams and dried them for winter food and trade. Prime traditional clamming areas were piled high with mounds of shucked razor clam shells.

The English sea captain George Dixon and his men devoured the bivalves while exploring and trading for sea otter pelts in the Northwest and Alaska over two summers in the late eighteenth century (they sensibly wintered in Hawaii). Other shellfish could be found, but the crew knew what they wanted to eat: razor clams. Dixon wrote, "[For a repast] our men preferred a large species of the Solen genus, which they got in quantity, and were easily discovered by their spouting up the water as the men walked over the sands where they inhabited.... The animal... is exceeding good food."

Dixon was the first to formally describe the Pacific razor clam, while sailing in Alaska's Cook Inlet in 1788, and he sketched the shell as well. References to the scientific name as "*Siliqua patula* (Dixon)" acknowledge his contribution.

The fur trappers and settlers who came after Dixon and pioneered the development of Washington's coast through the 1800s made use

Historic clamming on Copalis Beach, the diggers harnessed to long surf sacks. Courtesy Museum of the North Beach

of razor clams as a basic provision that could also be exchanged for goods at the local trading store.

Peter F. Halferty launched the era of commercial canning, which went on to thrive for half a century. Halferty began his career digging and pickling razor clams by beaches near the Columbia River, peddling his wares door to door in nearby Astoria. In 1894, he developed a special process for cooking and canning the clams, and he built a mini clam-canning empire with his sons, with plants in Westport, Aberdeen, Copalis, Moclips, all in Washington, as well as in Cordova, Alaska.

Halferty's Pioneer Brand clams were "pure, wholesome, appetizing; so different from the ordinary canned clams in cleanliness, richness and flavor," as the Pioneer Brand recipe booklet of 1911 declared. Halferty was a romantic as well as an entrepreneur, and he fancied himself an amateur scientist. He wrote heartfelt but often wacky descriptions of razor clam biology. He wondered why you so seldom see dead razor clams at the beach despite their abundance, and theorized that a clam, aware that its time was at hand, would leave

Digging razor clams and gathering Dungeness crabs in the early 1900s (harvested clams are in the wagon). Courtesy Museum of the North Beach

the beach and make its way past the breakers on its one leg, heading toward the sunset like a cowboy hero.

Halferty also attached strings to razor clams to observe their downward speed and trajectory, just like the biologist Harvey McMillin would do a few years later. To Halferty's credit, he offered a theory for how the clam moved up in the sand column as well as down. He wrote in a 1919 *Seattle Times* newspaper story that, to ascend from the depths, the razor clam somersaulted in the sand so that its digging foot was on top. Then it climbed to the surface just as it had descended, by extending its digger and pulling. At the surface it somersaulted again so as to feed with its siphon. When I read this explanation I burst out laughing. Imagining razor clams tumbling in the sand like circus performers boggled my mind. Still, some clams (not razors) do function somewhat in this way.

Other, far less inquisitive individuals quickly followed Halferty into the canning business. Soon, most every hamlet in Washington and Oregon near a razor clam beach had a canning operation, or several, as large-scale utilization of the resource took off. From the early 1900s on, razor clam canning was a thriving industry and the goods, generally chopped or minced, were as favored and ubiquitous as canned tuna is today. In 1915 Washington produced more than three million pounds of canned razor clams, a high-water mark. Labels were distinctive and colorful. Some assured customers that the cans were packed by white labor, a nod to the anti-Chinese sentiment of the time. Local whites and Native Americans supplied the clams, digging with special narrow-bladed shovels and collecting them in five-gallon kerosene kegs and wooden-wheeled handcarts, and later in long surf sacks harnessed to their bodies. When the sacks were full, the clammers dragged them to boxes, washtubs, and also horse-drawn carts and trucks, and ultimately to the buy shacks right on the beach. The money went for life's necessities. Diggers were preoccupied with the price paid by the buyers and also the exploits of champion diggers, who occasionally collected six hundred or even a thousand pounds on a good low tide, if they were skillful and found a productive bar, and dug like demons.

Canned razor clams were advertised in national magazines like *Good Housekeeping* and *Ladies' Home Journal*. Shellfish were an important part of the national diet, and canned razor clams proved popular for chowder and fritters and as an all-around cupboard staple—so much so that Washington and Oregon alone could not meet the demand, and canning operators expanded to Alaska.

Norah Berg, author with Charles Samuels of the memoir *Lady on the Beach*, published in 1952, portrayed her life and the coastal hamlet of Ocean City, Washington, around the Depression era and through World War II. She lived with her ex-marine husband Sarge in a shack just back from the dunes, and loved her seaside life among retired fruit pickers, drifters, fellow alcoholics, and assorted "misfits." Razor clamming was the principal local industry, she wrote, the staff of life for many, and "the folks in Ocean City talked of little else night and day, summer and winter."

The clams were a subsistence food dug for free, as well as a source of money. Local seasonal workers called bluebills arrived in winter and spring like the migratory greater scaup, a duck with a blue bill

Weighing clams for the canneries right on the beach. Courtesy Museum of the North Beach

and dark head. Field hands and fruit tramps from afar also came through to dig clams for the canneries, mostly from April to July, harvesting as much as possible during each clam tide. County officials established a public school for the razor clamming families in the outpost of Oyehut not far from what became Ocean Shores, utilizing a one-room shanty. Attendance varied from a crowded fifteen kids to nearly empty as the local population rose and fell according to the season. Classes were scheduled around clamming, and the teacher as well as the students hit the beaches morning, afternoon, or evening, depending on the tides. The evening digs were a scene of eerie beauty, according to a story from 1974, based on an interview with an old-timer who had attended the school, with "bobbing, weaving kerosene lanterns dotting the black night as families struggled against the economy for survival. . . . "

Some of the itinerant workers constructed shacks near the beach with scavenged wood. A few such outposts became encampments, with folks staying year round and perhaps hiding out, happy to forget their cares with surf fishing, razor clamming, and goose and duck hunting nearby. "Poor Man's Paradise" and "Ragamuffin's Riviera" were some of the nicknames for the camps, according to Norah Berg.

When I met Francis Rosander at the Quinault Indian Nation senior center, the elder launched into a barrage of anecdotes, tribal genealogies, and stories, all about razor clams. "We practically lived on razor clams, still do," he said. Rosander had worked as a cannery buyer, set up right at the beach to buy, and remembered one time when he had to offer fourteen cents per pound for clams, in order to outbid another buyer at the beach who had raised the going price. His boss, the cannery owner, was furious at the high per-pound payment. "Let me show you how you do this," he said. The next day, the cannery owner confronted the other buyer. "I've got deep pockets and I'm going to offer sixteen cents every day, until you are out of business. Do you understand me?" They quickly agreed on a lower price for all on the beach to follow. The owner turned to Rosander. "That's how you buy clams."

Rosander said some of the best diggers were the Native women, who could manage well over a couple of hundred pounds on a decent low tide. Helene Jake was notorious. No one could beat her.

A tribal enforcement officer listening to him reminisce leaned over and whispered in my ear, "Helene Jake was Bay Center Chinook. Like I am." Tribal pride runs deep, and everybody likes a champion razor clam digger.

Often overlooked are the people who labored in the canneries cleaning clams, typically women. Daisy Ackley kept a diary:

> MAY 7TH. Worked in the cannery today, came out "head cleaner" on first sink. Cleaned 1228 lbs. then worked on second sink a while and cleaned sixty-eight lbs. . . .
> MAY 10TH. Worked again today and cleaned 1567 lbs. clams. . . . One of the workers got one of his feet badly crushed necessitating the services of a physician. He will be laid off his regular duty for several days. . . .
> MAY 12TH. Cleaned 1500 lbs. clams and after supper did my washing, pretty good day's work for a scrub, (or runt).

MAY 14TH. Cleaned 1531 lbs. clams. Some old "hens" have been pretty quarrelsome and were pecking at each other on every occasion. None of them got their combs or wattles spurred, (but by all rights should have).

Cleaning 1500 pounds of razor clams by hand and knife in a shift is no trivial matter.

In the 1930s the smaller canneries started going out of business, not only because of the Depression, but because of competition from Dungeness crab fishers who wanted the clams for crab bait and bid up the price; the new technology of freezing helped make the perishable razor clam more practical as bait. Also, more and more diggers were taking clams for personal use, putting additional pressure on the commercial supply. Clarence Sigurdson, a cannery manager from a cannery family, dismissed these folks as interlopers and tourists. He complained that, at the beginning of the century, one team of horses and wagon with associated diggers was all that the diggers allowed on a clam bar, but in later years there could be "one or two hundred diggers on a bar. Mostly tourists."

Many of those "tourists" arrived by train, at least until the late 1930s, when roads and cars came to dominate. Until that time the Northern Pacific Railway ran to the seashore and up and down the coast, in some places with tracks right on the sand. On weekdays the railroad carried forest workers in and timber out, but on weekends the train brought as many as two thousand visitors to such places as Moclips, the town at the end of the line. They disembarked to enjoy car races on the beach, razor clamming, and hotels overlooking the waves. The Museum of the North Beach is celebrating the region's railroad heritage by constructing its new home as a replica of the Moclips train depot.

From the 1930s through the 1960s the cannery industry declined. During the 1940s clam stocks were low, leading to a commercial poundage quota for conservation purposes. At the same time, West Coast crabbers continued to expand operations, going farther and

A postcard in the shape of a razor clam, dated 1907. The verse promotes taking the railroad to Clatsop Beach, Oregon. Railroads such as the A & C, the Astoria and Columbia River Railroad, carried a multitude to the coast for seashore holidays before roads and cars became ubiquitous. Courtesy Pacific Shellfish Ephemera, Matt Winters Digital Collection

farther offshore and buying so many of the limited clams for bait that they drove up prices and undermined the consumer market. "Dear Madam," began a letter from the Razor Clam Canners Association to its customers, full of grievance, dated January 6, 1950:

> You are being denied the privilege of buying canned Minced Razor—a privilege that has been yours for many years. Here is why!
>
> The shocking situation that confronts this seafood delicacy—a highly desired human food—is that the bulk of the supply for Razor Clams taken from the Ocean Beaches in Washington has been used for Crab bait during the past two seasons.
>
> Bait buyers bid the price higher than the Canneries could afford to pay and still give you a reasonable price per can.

The letter urged readers to mail the enclosed postcard and tell Washington's governor to stop razor clams being diverted "to the lowly use of crab bait." The governor heard their pleas. The state sued to stop exports to California and Oregon of razor clams for bait, which accounted for some 30 percent of the commercial production. That legal effort failed in court. The razor clam canning industry was on the way out. The death knell sounded when Atlantic coast sea clams, mechanically dredged from the sea bottom, hit the market. Those clams were not as sweet and tasty as razor clams, but they were good enough and, not having to be dug and cleaned by hand, were less expensive. West Coast razor clam canneries couldn't compete.

Two Washingtonians tried to mechanize the West Coast razor clam harvest in 1910, hoping to revolutionize commercial clam digging and make their fortune. Lorenzo R. Gage, a log scaler on the Hoquiam River, along with a friend—George Croston, a post office night clerk—built the marvel in their spare time over the course of several years. The chassis was thirty feet long and sported three iron wheels each taller than a man, two wheels in the front and one in the back for steering. When they deemed the machine ready, they barged it through Grays Harbor and unloaded it near the razor clam beaches of Ocean Shores. Gage fired up the two gasoline engines and chugged along the beach and into the surf. The invention was, no doubt, a sight. It resembled an old-fashioned thresher, according to a newspaper report. A narrow scooping mechanism with screens unearthed the clams, which piled onto the deck. But the commercial razor clam diggers, who used shovels and who were relatively well organized and at times unionized, like their Industrial Workers of the World labor brethren—the Wobblies—raised a howl. Within three days the machine was back in Hoquiam, never to be used again, and eventually sold as junk. At the very next session the state legislature outlawed mechanical razor clamming. Only hand-operated implements were allowed, the lawmakers said, and that has been the rule ever since.

In Alaska, British Columbia, and Oregon, efforts to mechanize the harvest continued until the early 1960s. But the hydraulic dredges and pumps never worked well enough to overcome the economic

Postcard of a family razor clamming with dogs, circa 1970s. Courtesy Museum of the North Beach

challenge of cheaper clams from the Atlantic coast and Asia, and the machines were too indiscriminate, harvesting undersized clams and perhaps damaging the environment. At any rate, the mechanical equipment was never able to achieve the intended goals.

After World War II, propelled by growing prosperity and mobility, recreational razor clam digging zoomed in popularity. More and more people started to realize that the whole family could come by car to the seashore, enjoy a day at the beach, razor clam, and have a free meal besides. Biologists started counting digger trips to better manage the resource in the face of the burgeoning numbers. In 1950, there were 237,000 recreational digger trips in Washington, and by 1970 that number had nearly tripled, to 623,000.

Some recreational clammers were so enthused that they took out commercial licenses for a nominal fee so they could harvest without the annoyance of an eighteen-clam recreational bag limit. An astounding estimated 30 to 40 percent of the commercial landing actually went for personal use in the 1960s. It spoke to the outsized importance of the bivalve, and perhaps a certain libertarian streak. Northwesterners like their razor clams, and they like them in quantity, without restrictions or regulations.

Recognizing the economic realities and growing tourist value of the sport, the state closed its public beaches, one by one, to commercial razor clamming. The management areas of Long Beach and Twin Harbors were closed in 1950. Copalis was closed in 1960. The final razor clam management area, Mocrocks, was closed in 1968. Commercial harvest remained possible only in two places: the detached spits at the mouth of the Willapa Bay, reachable by boat through sometimes tricky water, and the modest beach on the Quinault Indian Nation reservation—that is, on tribal land and under tribal control.

1968—a landmark year in American history, with humans orbiting the moon and the counterculture in full bloom—was thus also a landmark year in razor clamming: all the razor clams on Washington's public beaches were for the first time reserved for the recreational fishery. No commercial harvest. Razor clamming belonged to the people. Just go to the beach and dig your limit, spring, summer, and early fall, no license required. And folks did, flocking in record numbers to places like Long Beach and the newly created Ocean Shores to dig their allotted eighteen clams. To top it off, a novel implement had been invented: the razor clamming tube. Center the tube over a clam show, lower it into the sand, and pull up the coring with clam within. Voilà. No need to master the sometimes-challenging shovel or get wet in the surf unless you wanted to. The tube made the learning curve quick and easy. Hundreds of thousands put on their beach finery and made their way to ocean beaches to participate in the fishery. The humble razor clam burrowed ever deeper into the Northwest psyche and self-definition.

It wasn't all fun and games. For some people, razor clamming was still more about family food than recreation. Dann Sears grew

The invention of the razor clam tube transformed recreational razor clamming. Simply center the tube over a show, rock or wiggle it into the sand, and lift. Courtesy WDFW

up in Aberdeen, and his dad toiled in the sawmills as an electrician. The workers were often going out on strike. He remembers his dad dragging him to the beach so the family could put dinner on the table. His father would wake him and his siblings at dawn. They'd head for the beach, where as often as not it was wet and cold. He'd put his arm into holes looking for clams, and get sand and water up his sleeve. And all he had to look forward to was spending the rest of the weekend cleaning the catch. When Sears moved away from Aberdeen he vowed that he would never dig or eat another razor clam. Though he returned to Aberdeen three decades later, becoming director and curator of the Aberdeen Museum of History, he has kept his vow.

More for everybody else, some would say.

As digger trips increased, recreational regulations evolved in tandem to help preserve the resource. In 1943 Washington State authorities implemented the rule that recreational diggers had to keep all the clams dug regardless of size or condition, to prevent wastage. In 1948 the bag limit decreased from thirty-six to twenty-four. The bag limit was further reduced in 1960 to eighteen, and finally, in 1973, to fifteen, where it remains today. In 1973 authorities also eliminated digging over the summer months to protect juvenile clams, safeguard ordinary beachgoers from cars, and push razor clammers to the coast in the economically slower non-summer months.

The fifteen-clam limit and lack of a summer season didn't derail the popularity of razor clamming. On the contrary, digger trips continued to surge. In the 1970s and early 1980s, a significant portion of the state's population was tearing up the beaches—more than 300,000 individuals, or about 7 percent of the state's population, in one memorable season. In 1977, and again in 1979—the year the state first implemented a razor clam license—the beaches saw nearly one million digger trips. An astounding multitude was digging holes in the sand and frying up the tasty clam. It no doubt seemed a marvel: you could razor clam in the morning on the coast and catch a production of Wagner's Ring Cycle at the newish Opera House in Seattle that same night. Razor clams were showing up on Seattle menus, too. *The Seattle Times* praised the chef at Nikko Restaurant, Seattle's first full-service sushi bar, for "making his customers razor-clam enthusiasts." Seattle restaurants such as Ivar's, a Northwest institution, and Charlie's, a popular Capitol Hill eatery, featured razor clam dishes in their advertisements. A food columnist opined that there was no Northwest regional cuisine with the possible exception of salmon cooked in traditional Indian style in front of an open fire, deviled Dungeness crab, and sautéed razor clams.

In these busy days of the late 1970s and early 1980s, no one had any idea of the disaster and altered landscape for razor clamming that lay on the horizon.

A VINTAGE CHOWDER
Makes 2 servings

The chowder recipe on this vintage razor clam can label calls for clams and potatoes but no milk or cream. Nowadays, such chowders are known as Rhode Island style, less well known than the familiar New England or Manhattan styles. The recipe reads:

> One slice bacon, cubed; fry until crisp, add pint potatoes chopped thin, one onion chopped fine, one small carrot, cubed, pinch of celery salt, sufficient water to cover and boil until tender; add contents of one can with five or six crackers, roll, season to taste. Serve hot.

"Crackers, roll" presumably means rolled—that is, crushed—crackers. The crackers were most likely saltines or some kind of soup cracker, another vestige of a mostly bygone era.

The last paragraph says, "Packed by white help under absolutely sanitary conditions," a nod to the anti-Chinese labor prejudice of the time.

Razor clam label from the commercial canning era, circa 1920, with colorful graphics and recipe. Courtesy Pacific Shellfish Ephemera, Matt Winters Digital Collection

"FRESH CLAM BALLS"
Makes 2 servings

Another older recipe, this one from the 1980s, adapted from Arlene Erickson in the Sharing Our Best *cookbook sponsored by the Grayland Orthopedic Auxiliary. It makes a tasty, simple fritter.*

- 2 tablespoons Bisquick biscuit mix or its equivalent
- ¼ cup Krusteaz bake and fry coating mix
- Pinch of garlic powder
- 1 tablespoon finely chopped shallot, optional
- 1 cup raw chopped razor clams, with their liquid
- Vegetable oil, for frying

Mix the Bisquick and Krusteaz mixes in a medium-sized bowl. Mix in the garlic powder, then the shallots and clams. Line a plate with paper towels. Heat ¼ inch oil in a medium-sized fry pan over medium-high heat. Drop heaping teaspoonfuls of the clam mixture into the hot oil and fry until the fritters are nicely browned, a couple of minutes on each side. (Alternatively, deep-fry the fritters at 350°F.) Transfer the finished fritters to a plate when cooked.

CHAPTER 6

THE ERA OF NIX AND DOMOIC ACID

HUMAN beings are not known for their self-control. When nature serves up a bounty of razor clams, it's hard to stop digging and follow the rules. Washington State fisheries authorities have chaperoned the beaches for more than a hundred years, using a basic strategy to preserve the resource for both recreational and commercial diggers: keep track of the clams and their removal, and set the total allowable catch low enough to assure their reproductive continuity. Since mature razor clams stay in one location, and don't move about except to go up and down, keeping tabs on them and their human exploiters is that much easier. But counting millions of clams buried in the sand isn't trivial, and human avarice and the vagaries of nature are hard to account for.

Authorities had to impose emergency conservation regulations as early as 1917. In that year L. H. Darwin, Washington's fish and game commissioner, slashed the commercial harvesting season from nine to three months when canned razor clam production plummeted. Cannery folks were furious, but they relaxed as the resource rebounded. As one of them said, "When the new law went into effect we were all swearing at Darwin. But now, since he has so forcibly

Two razor clammers on a quiet beach, headed to the surf amid reflected clouds

proved his point, we are swearing by him. The three-months law has undoubtedly saved the clam industry in this state."

Commercial and personal use regulations have always been intertwined, but personal-use clammers had it easy for the first three decades of the 1900s: no restrictions whatsoever. They could clam any day of the year with no limit. Finally, in 1929, just before the Great Depression, authorities put in place the first personal-use regulation, a thirty-six-clam limit, because of widespread abuses. Diggers were wasting great numbers of clams and also selling them illegally to canneries or other parties—"bootlegging," it was called, a reference to Prohibition.

After World War II, citizens turned from war to more pleasurable pursuits, like razor clamming. The number of digger trips started to increase, and as a consequence the number of clams that a personal-use (a.k.a. recreational) clammer was allowed to keep shrank, from thirty-six in 1948 to finally fifteen in 1973, where it remained. Digger trips were burgeoning and the season was nearly the entire year, but in the 1970s and early 1980s daily limits and good-sized clams were sometimes hard to come by. Biologists fretted about high levels of sorting and wastage as diggers threw away smaller clams. Worried that the brood stock was being depleted, they decreed frequent emergency closures as wastage at some beaches reached 40 percent.

Like wastage, poaching was high, with some people "double dipping"—that is, taking a limit and then going back and getting another. Poaching, of course, is hard to measure. You can't ask people about it; they won't tell you. You can't check the beach after a dig for evidence; there's nothing left behind. But razor clam biologists and authorities live in the coastal communities and know what's what, more or less. "Clam diggers have a different mentality," said Doug Simons, the state's chief shellfish biologist, in 1985. "Unlike elk hunters or fishermen, they figure that it is not a privilege but they're entitled to the clams."

Hard realities helped fuel the feeling of razor clam entitlement. Timber and salmon resources, key providers of livelihood for coastal communities, had diminished. Judge Boldt's 1974 ruling undid a historic wrong and the violation of tribal rights by Washington state agencies, some public leaders, and owners of industry, but it also dramatically reduced the available salmon for non-tribal fishers, and with declining habitat there weren't so many salmon to begin with. Timber jobs were disappearing due to the export of unprocessed logs to Japan and the rise of regulations protecting spotted owls and old-growth forest. All of this provided the explosive context as people went to the beach to dig razor clams. After filling up the car with ludicrously expensive post-1973 "Arab oil embargo" gasoline, nobody wanted to drive to the beach and come home without a mess of large clams.

Some blamed the small and seeming lack of clams on people coming from out of state and taking too many. But Alan Rammer, a state biologist and razor clam educator, retrieved and analyzed the hard-copy citations given out by game wardens—a labor of love before computers—and found that it was coastal residents who were the main culprits. "The worst offenders were us, the local yokels," Rammer explained in his educational evenings on the coast. Especially guilty were older folks who thought of the clams as a birthright akin to apple pie and the American flag. As often as not, they were the violators, with over-the-limit clams hidden in their waders, and the ones discarding little clams. Rammer spoke of watching a grandfather showing his granddaughter how to bury little clams. He confronted them and uncovered a hole filled with twenty-three little clams. The grandfather denied that the hole was theirs, but the granddaughter said, "We buried them, Grandpa."

Rammer wanted people to understand not only the razor clam's natural history and reproductive habits, but also why you couldn't sort your clams and put little ones back in the sand on your way to a fifteen-clam limit. The returned clams rarely live, he would explain, seeking to educate and, through that, change behavior to better preserve the resource.

Karen and I attended one of Rammer's sessions, and as it ended he offered the assembled some wheel-shaped hard candies. They were inscribed with the words "Conserve Razor Clams" in red letters. A little present to take home, to reinforce his message. People rushed to the table taking handfuls. "Just take one," Rammer was saying, barely audible above the crush. "They were expensive to make." Not a good sign, I thought.

In 1979, as the number of digger trips swelled to record levels, the state for the first time implemented a razor clam license requirement costing $2.50, to help with regulation, enforcement, and research. The imposition created a stir. Pay a license fee??!! This was not in the great tradition of Washington's long, flat beaches and meaty razor clams available without cost to all who were willing to grab a shovel or tube and face the elements. In an editorial, *The Seattle Times* lamented that "when one of the state's last free meals—the delicious razor clam for the unlicensed taking on ocean beaches—was withdrawn in 1979, there were understandable cries of anguish."

But clam lust was unquenchable and the license requirement didn't deter clammers a whit. The licenses sold handily and produced a pot of money. Biologists launched a hatchery program to help make up for humanity's overreach or what nature couldn't provide. Within two

Emergency closures often frustrated diggers in the 1970s and 1980s. Bob McCausland cartoon, courtesy Ruth McCausland

years, 80,000 quarter-inch-long clams were planted on Long Beach and Twin Harbors beaches, a considerable achievement. The expectation and hope was that 5 to 10 percent might reach adulthood.

The Seattle Times lauded the world's first hatchery-raised razor clams in 1981: "It's a start toward replenishing a dwindling clam population. It should be cheered by diggers who have labored fruitlessly for limits this spring."

Meanwhile, digging pressure stayed strong. There were some good clamming days, but also many days when the clamming wasn't so good. Regulators were almost certainly overcounting the number of clams and undercounting the amount taken by diggers at many beaches. They continued to manage with emergency closures, and "razor-clam-starved Washingtonians" endured shortened seasons.

Then things seemed to turn around. Beach monitoring over the summer of 1983 showed lots of clams. The state predicted that diggers would be up to their eyeballs in razor clams come the fall. The razor clam express train was back on track. Let the good times roll.

That turned out to be wrong. In the late summer of 1983 the millions of razor clams in Washington's sandy beaches inexplicably disappeared. It was as if a magician had stood on the shore, waved a magic wand, and made all the clams go away.

Alarmed authorities found a backhoe and dug a trench in the beach forty feet long and more than four feet deep, running the sand through a screen. They found a few clams where there should have been thousands. "I think we picked up a total of six clams," said shellfish manager Tom Northup. "I can't begin to describe what a shock it is."

The clam population dwindled from about 20 million in June, to 6 million in August, to 1.5 million by the end of 1983—a 90 to 95 percent reduction in just a few months.

Of course, there were doubters. People wondered why, if so many clams were dead, no shells were found. After all, 19 million shells couldn't just disappear. Yet there were almost no dead clam bodies or scattered clam shells. People wondered if the biologists really knew how to dig and count clams. They would smugly march out to the beach, only to come back shaking their heads, saying, "You're right, there are no clams there."

The state biologists themselves had doubts. Razor clam populations had always fluctuated, but never anything like this nightmare.

On December 9, 1983, the state canceled the razor clam season in its entirety. It was front-page news in coastal newspapers and *The Seattle Times*. Business owners moaned. Diggers mourned. The tens of thousands who had grown up razor clamming or who had learned to love the activity—and for whom razor clamming was Christmas, Easter, personal therapy, family vacation, and quintessential Northwest experience all rolled into one—had a collective nervous breakdown.

"I'll miss it as much as I'd miss my wife if she left town," said one coastal denizen.

"It's going to be a disaster down here, and I mean a disaster," said the mayor of Long Beach.

Officials managed to find a few dead clams and sent them to Ralph Elston, a shellfish disease specialist located in Sequim, Washington.

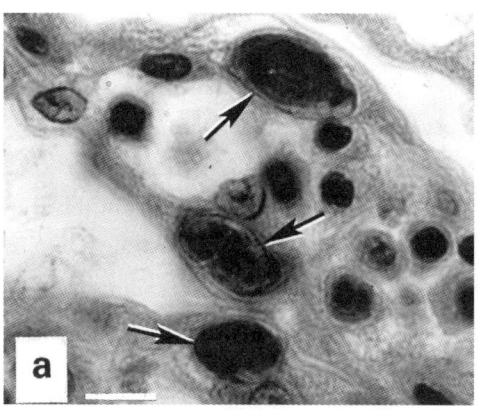

Cross-section of razor clam gill tissue with arrows pointing to invasive NIX bacteria. NIX massively infected Washington's razor clams in 1983 and caused them to die from a pneumonia-like disease. Courtesy Ralph Elston

Elston discovered a previously unknown microorganism in the gills. It was an infectious bacterium, primitive and gigantically sized—in fact, the largest bacterium ever identified. It attacked the nuclei of the razor clam's gill cells, causing them to swell and rupture. He called it Nuclear Inclusion Unknown, or NIX, a name that has stuck even through the present because NIX is very hard to culture and has not been studied enough to be given a proper scientific name. Gills are the breathing mechanism for clams, and as cells died and oxygen passageways clogged, the clam suffocated and became vulnerable to fatal secondary infections. A human equivalent would be pneumonia.

Folks feared that NIX might cause razor clams to disappear from Washington's beaches permanently. They feared that humans might become ill if they ate the shellfish. They feared that oysters, mussels, and other shellfish might start dying. They feared the economic harm to coastal communities.

Clamming stopped completely in 1984 and 1985, and Washington's rollicking post–World War II razor clamming era came to a halt. Razor clamming had gone on continuously for over a hundred years since the coming of the white man, and for thousands of years before that among Native people. The hiatus was unprecedented.

Authorities reacted by ramping up schemes to replenish the resource, with funding already started with money from the 1979 license fees. They outfitted the thirty-four-foot research boat *Molluscan* with a dredge and hoses, hoping to gather tiny baby razor clams offshore and seed depleted beaches. But the search for baby clams was fruitless. Then, on the morning of August 9, 1985, they stumbled on a concentration of baby clams just offshore, in a small canyon near Copalis Rocks, in twenty-five-foot-deep water. They vacuumed up "billions and billions" of the clams and raced to plant the weakest beaches. "It was like the answer to a prayer," said project lead Neil Rickard.

It had taken five years to design the dredge and procedures, and it was heartbreaking when the baby clams didn't make it. No one knew why. It wasn't NIX. Something special apparently happens as razor clams come ashore on their own that helps them survive. Vacuuming them up and distributing, even though the clams were on the verge of coming ashore, didn't work. "We came back and screened for clams, and there was nothing happening," said Alan Rammer, one of the biologists helping with the effort.

The offshore dredging effort stopped in 1986 or '87. The razor clam hatchery program, meantime, continued. Clams were growing prolifically, but at a certain point, just before they reached planting size, they started developing into a *J* or *S* shape. They lacked the art deco streamlining that helped normal razor clams propel themselves up and down so handily in the sand. "They couldn't get a straight clam," said Rammer. The hatchery program was also stopped around this time, though some research continued privately.

The worst fears about NIX didn't materialize. Other shellfish didn't die. Humans didn't become sick. Washington's razor clams weren't extirpated. It was never determined for sure if NIX was something new, or, more likely, had been lurking unnoticed till this concentrated outbreak. The best guess is that due to an El Niño year the oceans had warmed and triggered an explosion of the organism, with catastrophic results. NIX still lurks in the environment and to this day much more remains unknown about the disease than is under-

People feared that razor clamming was as extinct as the dodo bird after the NIX disease attacked razor clams in Washington in 1983. Bob McCausland cartoon, courtesy Ruth McCausland

stood, says Elston, the shellfish disease expert who conducted the initial investigation.

Everybody was stumped by the lack of shells on the beach. Although NIX had killed some 19 million razor clams in a matter of months, there were few signs of the die-off. Where were all the shells? Crabs in captivity were known to decimate a razor clam overnight, shell and all. But still, 19 million clams lost and virtually no shells?

Oddly, neighboring Oregon and British Columbia did not experience the same plague of mortality. They did find NIX in those regions, but in lower, nonfatal concentrations. And no NIX at all in the Queen Charlotte Islands (now called Haida Gwaii) or Alaska. Why was Washington—with the largest, most monitored razor clam fishery on the West Coast—so affected?

One theory was that freshwater rivers, like the Columbia, with their massive freshwater plumes thrusting into the ocean, separated razor populations into distinct stocks, and hence increased susceptibility to NIX. Biologists received funding for genetic studies and traveled from northern California to Alaska collecting DNA, but they found no discernible distinctions. Alaska, California, and Washington *Siliqua patula* were all the same population.

However, the biologists did discover something special about razor clams—that any two razor clams from a particular beach were genetically quite different. That was unusual for a lowly invertebrate. "They told us there was 'more difference between two clams on a beach than between two salmon in a river,' and salmon are vertebrates," says Dan Ayres, the current state razor clam manager, who was a state fisheries biologist during the NIX nightmare. The genetic diversity most likely helped razor clams to survive. The plague had come, but as in medieval times, some populace remained. No firm reason was determined as to why NIX was so deadly on the Washington coast and not in the vicinity of its immediate neighbors. Very possibly the apparent great density of baby clams on Washington's beaches that year, ordinarily a reason for happiness, promoted the growth and spread of the disease, just as contagions flourish in large, confined urban human populations.

The razor clams slowly came back, and by spring of 1986, more than two years after the NIX affliction, the beaches had recovered enough for the razor clamming fishery to cautiously open. Those for whom clamming was a necessity, part of their air and water, were grateful the clams were back at all. But razor clamming and its management were permanently changed. Before and after NIX—these are two distinct eras for razor clamming in Washington. Before NIX, there'd been long seasons, burgeoning numbers of diggers, and people mad for eating them. After NIX, there were far fewer clams, seasons were shortened, and digger trips were reduced by half or two-thirds, from 500,000 to 750,000 annually in the heyday years before 1983 to around 250,000 in the years after. Harvest totals were likewise greatly reduced, from 6 to 13 million clams to 2 to 3 million annually.

"We are now managing around NIX. There's no better description of our present posture," said state fisheries director Joe Blum, speaking to Aberdeen's *The Daily World* in 1989.

Gone were the open-every-day, month-after-month digging opportunities. In their place the state organized the year into truncated spring and fall seasons, with digging on odd-numbered days only. Razor clams, though resilient and fast growing, were newly appreciated as a vulnerable resource that needed more protection.

Nonetheless, the clams didn't dramatically rebound. "Our biggest fear is we are not seeing long-term recovery, even with the conservation measures we've taken to date," said Doug Simons, head of the state's razor clam program, in 1989. No one could explain why razor clam populations refused to recover.

Officials began managing the resource on a beach-by-beach basis to help maximize digging opportunities. This was an important change. Previously, all beaches were either open or closed, except for emergency closures. Now management areas were addressed individually: weak ones were closed and stronger ones opened. This approach provided more flexibility and nuance. You might have to drive a distance, but if you really wanted to dig, you could.

The public was deeply suspicious over the NIX closures and changes in the fishery. They wondered about the mystery of those missing clam shells. Many thought the "nuclear" in Nuclear Inclusion Unknown—NIX— meant radiation, like from a nuclear bomb, rather than referring to the nucleus, the spherical structure inside all cells that holds the genetic material. "People were very, very scared. Amazing how many people didn't know the center of the cell is called the nucleus," recalled Rammer, who became the state's razor clam educator in 1988 after having helped launch the program a couple of years earlier.

Rammer had plenty on his plate besides describing the clam's life cycle. Everywhere he went, people accused him—and the state—of plotting to keep people away from the resource. Sports club members glared and cursed at him. Rammer countered by showing photomicrographs of healthy razor clam gill tissue and then disfigured NIX-ruptured gill tissue. It quieted hostile audiences at his outreach meetings but didn't win them over.

Meanwhile, the hunger for razor clamming continued in the post-NIX, post–Boldt decision era, as a couple of new motel proprietors on the coast discovered.

Richard and Colette bought their four-unit motel resort and small RV park in 1990. Neither had ever owned a motel or even gone razor clamming. They just plunged in, intent on fleeing "polluted" Seattle and finding a rural Eden. "The digs were on odd days then. The state was trying to protect the resource," Colette remembered.

They took possession of the motel the last day of October, the 31st. The next day was November 1st. That meant two odd-numbered days in a row. They little anticipated how the back-to-back digging opportunity would create a frenzy their first days on the job.

"We were mobbed," Colette recalled. "We had people parked on the grass. We had the cars and RVs parked by the bathroom. We had them piggybacked by the fence. We didn't know it was illegal to have so many people. We just thought, they all want to clam, we'll pack them in."

Colette worried about her customers wandering about on the dark beach in the cold. She brewed a big pot of coffee to welcome them on their return. "Ha! They all had coolers with wine and beer. 'We're not cold,' they said. I didn't know it would be like that. They were all so happy."

One can only surmise that if her customers were happy, they must have gotten their clams.

Rammer ultimately had more to explain than just NIX, as another natural occurrence disrupted and altered razor clamming only five years after the NIX calamity.

It was November 1991, just before the popular Veterans Day razor clam dig. Frank Cox, the state marine toxin testing coordinator, had been temporarily reassigned to Long Beach to inspect oyster-processing plants. He was a little bored one evening, so he dug some razor clams for fun and sent them off to the state Department of Health lab for routine paralytic shellfish poisoning (PSP) testing, which was all the state tested for at the time.

A microbiologist named Gary Skow was on duty. He ground up the razor clam bodies, mixed the resultant slurry with a weak hydrochloric acid solution to mimic stomach acid, and then injected a precise amount into a mouse, per U.S. Food and Drug Administration (FDA) protocol. If the mouse died or started gasping for breath, it would be a sign of PSP.

The mouse didn't gasp for breath but started scratching its shoulder with its hind feet. Then it did some barrel rolls and expired.

Skow recognized the mortal gymnastics. He had been to a marine toxin conference in Sweden two years earlier and had heard about the world's first recorded outbreak of amnesiac shellfish poisoning (ASP) in eastern Canada in 1987. Over a hundred people had become ill, with three dying and fourteen suffering permanent brain damage. The health crisis was traced to eating blue mussels raised in the Gulf of Saint Lawrence. Eventually, researchers found the ultimate culprit: a bloom of plankton in the water that produced a biotoxin called domoic acid. The filter-feeding mussels concentrated the domoic acid as they fed on the plankton, and humans ingested it when they ate the mussels. The toxin causes human nerve cells to keep firing, resulting in illness if potent enough or even death. In mice it causes the peculiar antics that Skow observed in his laboratory.

Near panic ensued from Skow's discovery. It was fortunate that only one of Washington's razor clamming areas, Long Beach, was open; otherwise, the task of closing the beaches and alerting the public would have been overwhelming. Authorities didn't really know what domoic acid was or what effect it might have. All available personnel were called in to patrol the beaches and close the fishery, and tell people to throw away previously collected clams.

Health officials contacted all Long Beach residents to see if anybody had become sick. Cox remembers every one of the twenty-five possible victims he interviewed. The survey was complicated because there was also a flu bug going around. Ultimately, health officials determined that eleven people had mild symptoms of nausea, diarrhea, and vomiting from domoic acid poisoning, including one woman who had eaten sixty clams.

Three months later, in February 1992, the domoic acid levels showed no signs of declining. The clams themselves exhibited no harm from the toxin; only humans were affected. But the toxin was widespread in all the razor clam beaches, thus manifesting quite differently from paralytic shellfish poisoning, which, when high toxin levels forced closures for razor clams, was generally localized and also quickly purged, or depurated. As it turns out, razor clams are slow to depurate domoic acid from their tissue. As a result, Washington's beaches were closed to razor clamming for a year and didn't open again until November 1992. From a human point of view, it was as much of a disaster as NIX was just a few years earlier.

Closures due to high levels of domoic acid have occurred periodically ever since, including the entire seasons of 1998–1999 and 2002–2003. It hurts to have the beach full of healthy razor clams and not be allowed to dig.

Rammer had to educate his audiences about the new marine neurotoxin, domoic acid, as well as NIX. "Demonic" acid, he called it, for the way it sneaks into the brain like a ninja, mimicking a human neurotransmitter, and for the nasty damage it can cause: nausea, disorientation, permanent loss of short-term memory—hence the disorder's name, amnesiac shellfish poisoning—as well as coma and death.

Domoic acid is a naturally occurring toxin produced by the phytoplankton *Pseudo-nitzschia* (SUE-doh NICH-e-yah), and levels in razor clams can rise quickly when there's a bloom. In 2005, domoic acid spiked in razor clams from 11.5 to 68 parts per million in three days—"a huge jump," according to an Oregon state official, and zooming right through the safety threshold of 20 parts per million (ppm) at which point razor clamming is canceled.

Researchers, struggling to understand domoic acid's rapid and seemingly random appearances, collected water samples and studied satellite imagery of ocean chlorophyll levels. Eventually, three scientists, Vera Trainer, with the National Marine Fisheries Service, and Barbara Hickey and Rita Horner, with the University of Washington's School of Oceanography, proposed a solution. Some ten years after the toxins first appearance in the Northwest, they identified the gigantic circular eddy near the mouth of the Strait of Juan de Fuca, the waterway separating Washington State from British Columbia, as the source of *Pseudo-nitzschia* in the fall season.

The eddy is a hotspot for *Pseudo-nitzschia* blooms, they said, and those blooms, for reasons not yet fathomed, sometimes produce domoic acid. Then, if a particular, Rube Goldberg–like sequence of wind and weather patterns occurs, strands of these harmful algae break off and move south, getting pushed to the coastline, where the razor clams ingest them. If domoic acid levels in the clams cross 20 ppm, the beaches are closed.

In spring, currents and winds are different. The blooms of *Pseudo-nitzschia* originate from the south at a hot spot on Heceta Bank off the Oregon coast and reach Washington's razor clams only during strong northerly storms.

The Columbia River plume is a variable in these scenarios, a vast pool of freshwater, up to 50 miles wide and 150 miles long, pushing into the ocean. Sometimes this freshwater guards the coast and keeps *Pseudo-nitzschia* blooms offshore, and other times it acts like a funnel, channeling the blooms right to the shore and the razor clams.

Researchers are starting to place automated labs off the coast of Washington and other states so that harmful algal blooms, or HABs, such as from *Pseudo-nitzschia,* might be tracked and predicted much like the weather, perhaps as much as two weeks in advance. Such forecasts could help maximize shellfish harvests and avoid abrupt closures and threats to human health.

But that's the future. The reality now is that razor clam digs are sometimes canceled with barely a day's notice. When that happens it's like an escalator suddenly halting, and people's plans go every which way. Researchers at the University of Washington found that the amount spent in the 2007–2008 razor clamming year was about $90 per digger per day, or about $24 million over the entire season. The money was spent on lodging, restaurants, groceries, gas, and gifts, and it rippled through the local economy. A lost season, or even a few weekend closures, can severely cost the coastal economy, as razor clammers cancel motel reservations and trips. In the fifteen-year period from 1997 to 2013 the health department canceled nearly 25 percent of all planned razor clam days due to marine toxins, primarily domoic acid. However you slice the economic model, that's a lot of financial unhappiness. And razor clammers are miserable, too, thinking about all those fat clams they can't harvest.

From the 1980s until the 2012–2013 season, annual digger trips hovered at around 250,000 per year as razor clammers adjusted to the post-NIX regime. The new normal was characterized by more regulation, reduced razor clamming days, and the possibility of domoic acid closures. Authorities abandoned the loathed odd-days-only plan in 1996, and in its place allowed clamming digs on a few continuous days during the best low tide series of each month, from October through May. This eight-month season was a much more desirable regime for diggers and businesses alike.

Razor clamming remained an easy and popular connection to the natural world. A vast array of folks still put aside distractions and felt the tug of the tides, gathered with friends at the seashore, and came

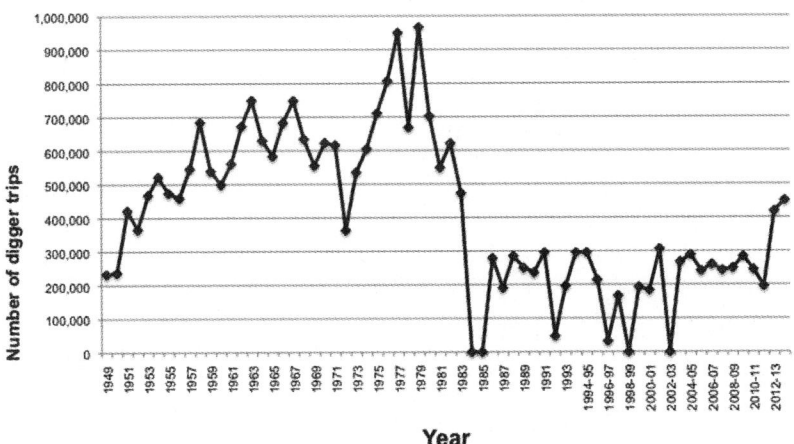

RAZOR CLAM DIGGER TRIPS PER YEAR, 1949-2013
NIX changed razor clamming in Washington. Digger trips were trending upward until the NIX disease nearly wiped out the clams in 1983. The clams didn't fully recover, for reasons not understood, and the number of digger trips was much reduced. The years of zero digger trips in the chart, in 1991, 1998, and 2002, were due to the marine biotoxin domoic acid closing the beaches. The low digger trip number in 1996-97 was due to reduced clam populations, most likely caused by NIX.

home with a bag of booty. Coastal residents still filled the freezer and put up clams. Parents still took their children, and vice versa. It was a smaller number compared to the heyday years of the 1970s, but thousands and thousands still charged the surf and had fun getting cold, wet, and sandy. Cars and people still crowded the beach on nice weekends in spring. Despite all, the phenomenon was strong.

Then, in 2012, thirty years after the NIX catastrophe, the status quo for no discernible reason began to change. Razor clam populations started to increase, to general astonishment. Digger trips in 2013–2014 were nearly 500,000, almost double previous years, as people responded to increased digging opportunities. The beaches were full of healthy clams. In spring they bulged with spawn, fat as knockwurst, and there were plenty of them. The jinx that began in 1983 with the arrival of NIX seemed to have ended. Everyone said it was the best clamming in thirty years, and it was true.

A clammer wiggling in a tube in the post-NIX era in 2006

Meanwhile, in Alaska, along the east side of Cook Inlet, the locus for recreational razor clamming there, the situation changed in a different way: the bivalves suddenly started failing to replenish themselves. Managers dropped the recreational limit from sixty to twenty-five in 2013, and then closed all beaches in 2015 due to a lack of both mature and juvenile razor clams. They don't know the cause. Perhaps environmental reasons, or a parasite researchers discovered in the clam's reproductive organs. Alaskan biologists are trying to sort it out. Meanwhile, local razor clam devotees are chartering boats and planes and making the long journey to the west side of Cook Inlet to get their fix. The clams there are still healthy and robust.

Razor clam populations vary unpredictably. Setbacks can appear without warning. Enjoy them when you can, and don't take them for granted.

"CLAMSHELL RAILROAD" CLAMS CHOWDER
Makes 4 servings

Chef Michael Lalewicz of the Depot Restaurant in Long Beach says there are two recipes the restaurant can never take off the menu, and this chowder is one of them. The name of the recipe, "Clamshell Railroad," refers to the Ilwaco Railway and Navigation Company, which ran a narrow-gauge railroad on Long Beach Peninsula until 1930.

Lalewicz uses local steamer clams as well as razor clams to double up on the clam flavor. With razor clams in the ocean beaches on one side and steamer clams in Willapa Bay on the other, the Long Beach Peninsula is indeed a fortunate place. (The Willapa Bay flats are private, though, so no public collecting of steamer clams is allowed.)

- 3 tablespoons chopped garlic
- 1 large leek, finely diced
- 2 stalks celery, finely diced
- 2 tablespoons champagne vinegar
- 1 cup dry white wine, such as Pinot Gris
- 2 tablespoons unsalted butter
- 1 teaspoon ground white pepper
- 2 tablespoons all-purpose flour
- 2 cups heavy cream
- 2 cups whole milk
- 1 large russet potato, diced, cooked in 3 cups salted water until tender
- 4 ounces (about 16) live Willapa Bay steamer clams, rinsed
- 1 cup chopped canned razor clams, with their liquid
- Salt and freshly ground black pepper
- 2 to 3 tablespoons chopped Italian flat-leaf parsley

In a heavy pot over low heat, place the garlic, leek, celery, vinegar, wine, butter, and white pepper. Stirring occasionally, simmer the mixture until the wine has evaporated, about 5 minutes. Mix in the flour with a wooden spoon until incorporated. Add the cream and milk, turn up the heat to medium-high, and bring to a boil. Simmer for two to three minutes, long enough for the liquid to thicken. Remove from the heat. Add the potato to the pot, along with the steamers and razor clams with their juice. Cover and return the pot to a low simmer. When the clam shells open, after a couple of minutes, the chowder is ready. Add salt and pepper to taste, garnish with the parsley, and serve.

Note: Lalewicz says you can't simply substitute fresh razor clams when making this chowder. The canned razor clams, which he buys wholesale, have liquid from the commercial canning process with a particular flavor, and the clams are essentially tenderized from being treated with salt and steamed and cooked before canning. As a workaround, he suggests using a bottle of clam juice to balance out the flavor and consistency, and adding chopped fresh razor clams, as many as you like—preferably lots—just before serving.

CHAPTER 7

PUMPING AND COUNTING

With his low-key, diplomatic manner, mat of white hair, and bemused smile, Dan Ayres makes an unlikely hero—or villain—of razor clamming, but he's been forced into both roles as the key figure overseeing Washington's razor clam harvest since around 2000. He's a minor celebrity at the coast, buttonholed on the beach for autographs and serving as judge for cooking contests at razor clam festivals. Studying zoology at the University of Washington certainly didn't prepare him for such roles. But being the resource manager for razor clams involves politics and psychology as much as biology. In a way, Ayres is like the Easter Bunny, doling out a finite number of Easter eggs every year, never knowing how many eggs he might have or when they might suddenly disappear, while a group of eager children look on, waiting for the signal to begin, anxious to get started, fearing the worst—No Easter egg hunt! Canceled due to lack of Easter eggs! And the parents, a.k.a. coastal businesses, are standing behind the kids with murder in their eyes.

If you are going to dole out Easter eggs, you had better know how many you have in your basket. Ayres joined the state fisheries department in 1980 and some ten years later saw a newfangled way for counting razor clams demonstrated in Alaska. He was enthralled and immediately wanted to bring the "pumped-area method" to

A Fish and Wildlife staff person using a water wand and the "pumped-area method" to count clams on Copalis Beach

Washington. The basics were simple: Use a pumped jet of water to liquefy a defined circle of sand, and count the clams that float up in the resulting hole. Then do this over and over along a line from the upper beach all the way to the surf, thus determining an average density of clams, and finally multiplying that density by the total beach area. Presto, an extrapolated and reasonably accurate population count. With such a count, biologists could more readily apply an exploitation rate and thus better manage the resource that so many thousands of people wanted to dig. It was doubly critical to have an accurate count after the Quinault Indian Nation gained the right to half the clams in their usual and accustomed places in 1994, thanks to the Rafeedie decision. Until the state implemented the pumped-area method in 1997, Ayres said, "We were crying the blues of how our data was collected. We always knew how many diggers, but never the actual number of clams."

I saw the pumped-area method in operation early one summer morning. The state's vehicles cast long shadows in the slanting light of dawn. Down at the surf a stout hose extended from the ocean, thick as a fire hose. Sourcing water from the ocean was unusual, said Clayton Parson, the lead technician, but on this day there were no convenient lagoons (that is, ponds of water left behind on the beach by the outgoing tide). So they were getting water directly from the Pacific Ocean.

Parson, forty-four, with a shock of close-cropped hair and plenty of enthusiasm, has been doing razor clam work for more than two decades. He grew up in the area and, as a kid, went razor clamming with his dad in the wee hours before school. As it turned out, those early morning jaunts jump-started his career. Back in the day, the state used a stock assessment method called mark and recapture, which required an experienced clam digger. Parson, at age nineteen, understood the tao of the clam shovel, and he was hired.

Mark and recapture is a standard methodology that generates data about animal populations almost like magic. A portion of a population is captured, then marked and released; a subsequent recapture effort snares both marked and unmarked individuals, and based on the proportion between the two groups the total population size can be estimated. Such a clever technique to determine relative abundance. Applying this method to razor clams, Parson's crew would dig twenty or thirty clams, engrave them with an identifying letter and number, and then plant them back in the sand in a delineated plot. At the next low tide cycle, usually two weeks later, they would return to dig in that same plot until they recovered at least 20 percent of the marked clams—that is, four to six clams. They did this at multiple locations.

Unfortunately, the process was not as accurate as the razor clam managers would have liked. It was not a true population count, and it was highly dependent on one particular assumption: that all twenty or thirty of the marked and replanted clams were still in place in the sand. As it happens, this was not necessarily the case. Seagulls and especially crows are clever animals. They soon learned that a truck on the beach could mean a meal. Many a day found Parson running down the beach shaking his shovel at a bird as it made off with a marked clam.

Part of the challenge was that clams need time to establish themselves in their sand silos when replanted. That silo is where the clam spends its life ascending and descending, and it becomes softer than the surrounding sand, so the clams can dig down faster. But the crews were replacing the clams into virgin sand with no well-traveled corridor, and it was time-consuming and difficult to plant them at any depth.

If even one marked clam went missing in the mark-and-recapture method, the analysis could be skewed. Nevertheless, mark and recapture provided a year-to-year comparison for how the clams were doing and revealed whether populations had gone up or down. It was the basis for management decisions for many decades.

As the pumped-area method was phased in, both methodologies were used for a while, to test the new technique and see if there was some way to equate the two data sets. But mark-and-recapture

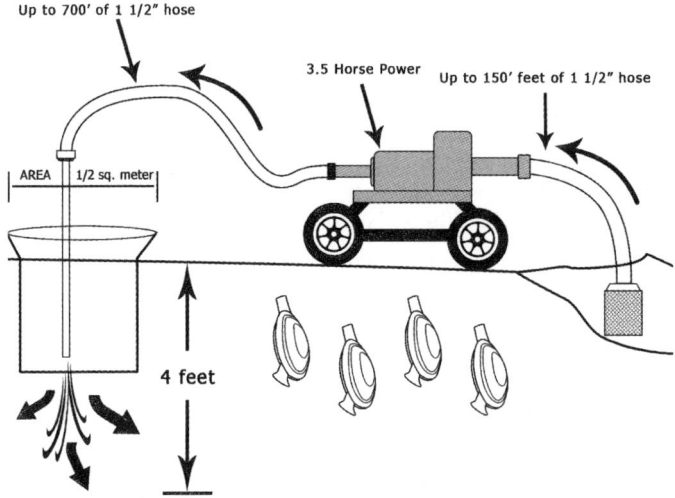

A beefy pump powers the water wand. Water is sourced from "lagoons"—pools of water left behind by the receding tide—or the ocean, if no lagoons are available.

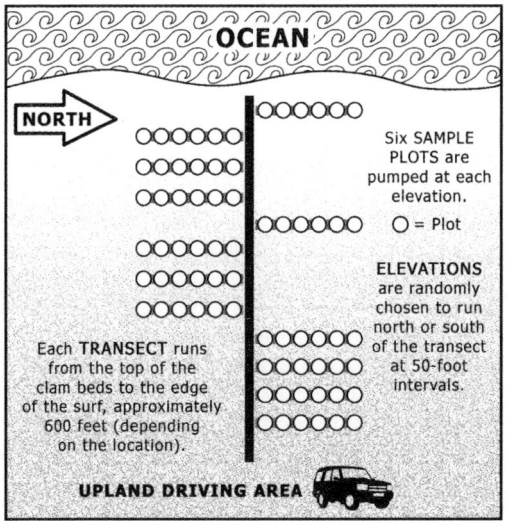

In the pumped-area method, biologists gauge the number of clams in the beach by excavating a sequence of holes, called plots, to determine the average density, and then multiplying that density by the total beach area. Redrawn graphic from Washington State Department of Fish and Wildlife.

data proved too variable, and sustaining two labor-intensive efforts quickly became untenable.

To excavate a hole, called a plot, using the pumped-area method, razor clam technicians first set an aluminum mesh drum—it looks like the inside of a washing machine—into the sand. They then scour the sand circumscribed by the drum with a water wand powered by a beefy gas pump. They scour till the holes reach at least four feet deep, below the maximum depth at which clams are found. A cheap digital watch strapped to the wand buzzes at three minutes; they time themselves to encourage efficiency.

The crew digs along lines from the upper beach all the way to the low tide, a length of five hundred to six hundred feet. They establish a starting line at each management area through a process that ensures randomness, and then measure each additional line a mile distant. Since there are fifty-three miles of razor clam beach, the crew digs along fifty-three lines, plus a few more in special areas. They mark each line, called a transect, at fifty-foot intervals, and at each of these marks, about ten, they dig six holes. So, roughly sixty holes per transect. They like to complete a transect in one low tide, and that takes a lot of hustle. It's not possible if each hole takes much more than three minutes.

I watched the state's razor clam workers blast hole after hole and count every clam within the ring, a half meter square in area. It was a sunny Monday morning, and the beach at dawn couldn't have been more pleasant. Snow-capped mountains crested over the bluffs to the north. The crew had been working through the night, taking advantage of the low tide. It was impressive seeing them study the pooled water in each hole, using their hands to screen through wood chips and floating debris, looking for even the tiniest clams, half the size of a pinkie nail. The priesthood of data collection is doubtless tedious at times, but the workers were thorough, measuring and recording every clam that churned to the surface. They know the importance of detail. The whine and chug of the gas motor blended with the

Fish and Wildlife staff wrangle hoses and dig holes to implement the pumped-area method. The work takes place over the summer during the best low tides, sometimes in the middle of the night and sometimes during the day.

rumble of the surf. The tide was still going out and the team was following it down. They were in constant motion: setting up, moving the hose, rolling the water pump on its custom-built metal cart, blasting holes—the three-minute drill—measuring clams, returning them into the firming sand, two folks picking up the ring and laying it down one ring diameter away, ready to pump the next hole. They moved with the efficiency of a racing car team changing tires. Pump, measure the clams, put them back.

Nearly every hole turned up clams. Big ones ready for harvest in the fall, and small ones that would be ready to harvest after a year of plankton feeding and growth. Very auspicious. Whatever the superstructures of regulations and politics, the basic fundamental for a happy year of clamming was a good number of clams. Too few clams, no harvest. Lots of clams, glory and hallelujah.

It takes most of the summer to do the sampling. By the end of August the assessment teams had made Swiss cheese of all Washington's razor clamming beaches. The results were turned into charts showing the density of clams in each of the five management areas. Razor clam populations fluctuate naturally, and the charts resembled the nearby Olympic Mountains, all peaks and valleys. Later, Ayres would get together with other stakeholders, including his tribal counterparts, and use these charts to determine the number of razor clamming dates in the upcoming year.

Ayres is proud of the pumped-area method, which transformed razor clam management into something much more precise and surefooted. He takes his work stewarding the razor clams personally, given that he grew up in the coastal city of Aberdeen. His parents were both "crazy diggers" who loved to dig and consume razor clams. His grandparents told him stories of surviving the Great Depression by digging and eating razor clams, and trading them for potatoes. Razor clams have burrowed deeply into the coastal psyche.

When Ayres joined the state fisheries department in 1980, he first worked on razor clams, then bottom fish for nine years, before returning in 1989 to razor clams. He was promoted to razor clam manager in 2001, originally reluctant to take the position for fear it would ruin his pleasure in the activity. But, ultimately, he wanted to help the tradition continue and provide a legacy to his children.

One of his first actions as manager was to launch an investigation into razor clam mortality and growth. This would prove to be almost as significant as the pumped-area method for putting maximum clams into harvesters' buckets. The undertaking was a bold move because the department had been restructured and trimmed; when promoted to manager, Ayres was given responsibility not only for razor clams but for crab and shrimp as well, and at the same time both budget and staff were reduced.

Nonetheless, the study was undertaken. It made use of three razor clam sanctuaries: quarter-mile-long sections at Long Beach, Twin Harbors, and Copalis that had been set aside by the state legislature in 1980 for research. Ayres engaged diggers to remove as many clams as they could in half of each reserve. Then the biologists watched how those depleted areas repopulated. As it turned out, the clams grew so fast that the two halves looked the same within two or three years. "It was pretty amazing how quickly the harvested area recovered," Ayres says.

These early results led the biologists and a staff biometrician named Henry Cheng to redesign the study with an increased focus on growth. They dug over one thousand clams. They etched the larger clams with an identifying number, just as had been done a few years earlier for mark-and-recapture population counts. On the smaller clams, with shells far too delicate for etching, they glued tags—the kind of mini-transponders injected into salmon snouts to register an identification when scanned with a reader. The tags were each a half inch in length, and twenty together weighed only as much as a dime. Nonetheless, it was a heavy burden for a tiny clam, and only those just over an inch long could support the load. The staff put all the marked clams, big and small, back in the sand, like returning babies to the cradle.

The department conducted the study over five years, going back every quarter to dig up the very same clams over and over. Sometimes they'd find people digging in the reserve during a recreational dig, somehow overlooking the signs and poles that marked the sanctuary boundaries. "We got pretty darn testy when we'd find somebody digging up our data," says Ayres.

As the study went on, clams died or disappeared, naturally or otherwise, and each time a clam was measured it became more valuable. At the end of the five years there weren't many clams left to study, but the data was complete enough for the department to realize that razor clams in Washington grew more quickly than the literature had said, reaching four inches in eighteen months, not two years, as had previously been thought. Four inches is about what most clammers consider the minimum size they like to bother with, while three inches, what biologists call recruit size, is when clams typically become visible as shows.

The growth study ended in 2009, and Cheng—a "gifted shellfish statistician," in Ayres's words—did a technical analysis, never published, showing that, given successful spawning and setting, harvest was not the driving factor in population densities. The bottom line was that harvesting could be done at higher rates.

Cheng designed a variable exploitation rate table to take advantage of the situation. When there were a lot of clams on a particular beach, the exploitation rate could be increased to as high as 40 percent. Use them or lose them. When clams were doing poorly, the table dictated that the exploitation rate should be reduced to allow populations to recover.

In 1997, when the department implemented the pumped-area method for population assessment, it was using a fixed exploitation rate of 25 percent. In 2006, with the pumped-area method providing better information about clam density, that fixed rate went to 30 percent. Beginning in 2012–2013, with the new variable rate table in hand, the exploitation rate went to the maximum of 40 percent at some beaches, because, coincidentally with the development of the table, there were sizable increases in the razor clam population.

The difference between a 30 percent and a 40 percent exploitation rate is large and means many more harvest days. In 2013, the department harvested at 40 percent at Twin Harbors. Authorities crammed in 105 days of digging opportunities, but even so, all the allocated clams were not taken.

Any population assessment and management method has uncertainty. There are margins of error, human mistakes, and other vagaries. Occasionally these can be large; a simple algebraic error discovered in the standard formula around 2013 led to red faces and the humbling realization that, in some cases, and going back about fifteen years, the department was undercounting the number of clams taken by diggers, sometimes by a significant percentage, as much as 20 or 30 percent or more. Absolute numbers are not necessarily critical as long as the clams and clam diggers are prospering year to year, but the state had to negotiate a plan with Indian tribes to equalize the imbalance in harvest totals.

Overall, Ayres says he has great confidence in the current management direction, because the densities of razor clams in the reserves are about the same as those not in the reserves. Harvest is not driving the population densities. Establishing those reserves in 1980 as a reality check and place to experiment was certainly one of the most sensible things ever done in Washington's razor clam management history.

Some think the state razor clam managers are allowing too aggressive a harvest, while others think that the exploitation rate could be much higher, 50 percent or even up to 70 percent. The latter group would like to see lots of three-consecutive-day openings to help pump money into the coastal economy. "Fish and Wildlife's clam experts, led by Dan Ayres, are knowledgeable, friendly and dedicated—and mistaken about how many clams must remain unharvested each year to ensure perpetuation of a healthy future population," wrote one critic in *The Chinook Observer*, a weekly newspaper serving Long Beach Peninsula and vicinity.

Even if the clams were overharvested, detractors say, it's not a problem, because plenty of razor clams live beyond the intertidal zone—that is, in sand rarely or never exposed at low tide—and thus are a fail-safe spawning stock.

Ayres doesn't think that. In summer, taking advantage of the extraordinarily low tides that occasionally occur in that season, he walks out to sand that is almost always underwater. If clams used this subtidal environment, you'd expect to hit a mother lode of clams. But over and over Ayres says he finds only a few. So he doesn't think razor clams populate the subtidal region in any quantity.

Ayres has a theory as to why this is the case. It's about food. Razor clams prefer the intertidal environment because low tide brings the plankton right to the razor clam's siphon, like a mother spoon-feeding her progeny. Subtidal clams would have to depend on plankton drifting down to the bottom, a much less desirable place at the table.

Crab fishers sometimes report finding razor clams in their crab pots when they pull them up from the ocean floor. Dale Beasley, president of the Columbia River crab fisheries organization, says he's brought up razor clams while crabbing fifteen miles offshore in three hundred feet of water. He says the hungry trapped crabs yank clams right out of the sand. The implication is that there are plenty of razor clams everywhere. Biologists generally consider these deep subtidal razor clams a different species, though, named *Siliqua sloati*, thinner than *Siliqua patula* and with a maximum length of four inches. But such matters, like the anecdotal reports of crab fishers, have not been much studied.

Knowing how many clams live in the sand is just half the management battle. Officials like Ayres also have to know how many people are clamming and how many clams they take. Since 1946 department staff have gone to the beach and counted recreational diggers literally one by one, with clickers. Other techniques have been tried, including flying over and tabulating from video, but none worked very well.

There are five management areas separated by rivers, bays, and land. Counting diggers is as logistically demanding as counting clams. Nowadays two staff are assigned to every management area at nearly every dig. At what they estimate to be the time of maximum digger effort, they drive slowly from one end of the beach to the other, clickers in hand. The driver counts the people on the upper beach near the parked cars, while the passenger counts the diggers down by the surf, working the clicker about as fast as a hand can manage on a busy day. "Our thumbs do sometimes get tired," says Parson. I looked at his hands to see if one thumb has grown exces-

Five happy clams signal a good season in 1994. Cartoon by Bob McCausland, courtesy Ruth McCausland

sively large, like a crab with one giant claw, but no—both thumbs looked the same.

They apply an expansion factor to the clicker count to estimate the total number of diggers for the entire low tide period. They also interview razor clammers to gauge digging success. On a good day, most everybody might have a limit of fifteen clams. If the rain is pouring down, or if the clams are off partying and not showing, the average creel might be just two or three clams.

The beach is a wild and untrammeled place, but biologists put on their chaperone hats and keep a close eye on both their human and mollusk charges. This is an intensely monitored fishery. They count the clams in the beach. They count the people digging. From time to time they count the cars ingressing and egressing at beach access roads, and when there's time they count the wastage, poking into holes looking for discarded or overlooked clams.

Together, these efforts put razor clam management on a firmer biological basis in the post-NIX era. Knowing the number of clams in the beach through the pumped-area method and having the variable exploitation table are Ayres's major technical contributions.

Every razor clam manager faces one central question every year: how to take "the maximum number of clams without injury to the beds," as the biologist Harvey McMillin put it in 1924. Under Ayres's stewardship, answering that question has become more matter of fact.

Of course, managers can't control the clams. Clams thrive or they don't thrive. But managers can regulate people and the schedule of digging opportunities, and consult with the public for input regarding the when and how. Nowadays the digs are distributed throughout the fall-to-spring season, providing varied digging experiences and a tolerable calendar for coastal businesses. There haven't been emergency closures in recent years due to lack of clams, and the clams have been reasonably sized. If there are still allocated clams at the end of the spring season, digging days are added. Relationships between tribal and nontribal diggers who share the harvests are good. Perhaps it's a conservative regime, but it's regular, and most people are happy enough.

Still, some just can't be dragged to the beach no matter how friendly the calendar or how big or plentiful the clams. My friend Jamie had never been razor clamming, so I called him with an invite.

"Do you wear clothes to protect yourself?" he asked. "Rain jacket, Gore-Tex, boots, to keep the sand off? I don't think I'd like having my arm in the wet sand. Ick."

"You can't wear too much," I said. "It's pretty physical. You have to move around."

"How do you keep the sand out of the car?"

"You don't. Sand gets in everything. It's a different world and there's just no resisting it."

"I'll only go if I can take a hot shower and throw away my clothes."

"Fine. It's a proxy for nature's abundance. Really, it's hopeful. A positive thing."

"Sand, cold, and touch the universe. . . . Well, good for city folk, I guess. But I don't think so."

DAN'S LOW-FAT RAZOR CLAM CHOWDER
Makes 6 servings

Dan Ayres, Washington's coastal shellfish manager, provided this recipe, which eschews salt pork, bacon, butter, and cream for a low-fat chowder. The use of buttermilk provides a distinct tang. Ayres says, "This is a very forgiving recipe, so feel free to add more or less of these ingredients as you choose. Like my mother did, I always have home-cooked canned razor clams on hand for soup and other recipes. They are tender, require almost no additional cooking and have a wonderful 'clammy' liquid that you want to be sure to include in your chowder. My motto with razor clam chowder is the more clams the better, so don't be afraid to add more than is listed here."

Ayres grows his own vegetables, so he generally has a supply of leeks and potatoes on hand in addition to the razor clams. This chowder is comparatively thin.

- 2 cups diced leeks or onions
- 2 cups Yellow Finn or Yukon Gold potatoes, cut into ¼- to ½-inch cubes
- 1 tablespoon olive or vegetable oil
- 3 cloves chopped garlic
- 4 cups canned razor clams, chopped, with their liquid, or 10 medium-sized fresh or previously frozen razor clams, chopped
- 4 cups low-fat buttermilk
- 1 (12-ounce) can evaporated milk
- 2 cups chicken broth, plus more as needed
- 1 teaspoon Tabasco, sriracha, or other hot sauce, plus more as needed (optional)
- Salt and freshly ground black pepper

In a large cast-iron Dutch oven or similar-sized soup pot, sauté the leeks and potatoes in oil over medium heat until they just begin to brown, 4 minutes or longer. Add the garlic and sauté another minute, until translucent. If you are using canned clams, add them to the sautéed ingredients along with the buttermilk, evaporated milk, chicken stock, and Tabasco. If you are using fresh or previously frozen clams, add them to the sautéed ingredients and sauté for another 3 to 5 minutes, then add the buttermilk, evaporated milk, chicken stock, and Tabasco.

Stir well and cook just below a simmer (do not boil) for a few more minutes, or until the potatoes are tender and easily pierced with a fork. Add salt and pepper to taste and serve immediately.

LEE'S RAZOR CLAM CHOWDER
Makes 8 to 10 servings

Lee Marriott is the director of the Museum of the North Beach in Moclips. Artifacts at the museum include railroad memorabilia, vintage razor clam shovels and surf sacks, and plenty of historic photos.

Marriott likes to freeze his razor clam catch in bags filled with water. This reduces the chance of freezer burn and, when defrosted, provides liquid to be turned into soup.

Marriott separates the razor neck from the body and grinds it the time-honored way, in a meat grinder. (A food processor or fine chop will do as well.) He likes to use a mixture of frozen ground-up necks and fresh diggers in his chowder, saving most of the clam bodies to fry. (To fry, he dips them in a mixture of half-and-half and beaten egg, dredges in seasoned flour, redips and dredges in panko mixed with dried basil, and then fries in butter, adding chopped garlic halfway through cooking.)

Along with reserved razor clam liquid, bottled clam juice, and a modest amount of half-and-half, Marriott's chowder uses HonDashi, which is an instant form of Japanese fish soup stock made from dried bonito flakes. Basil and Worcestershire sauce round out the flavors.

The recipe calls for the potatoes to be diced into two sizes, pretty small and a little larger. The smaller dice breaks down entirely in the cooking, thickening the chowder. This chowder is even better the next day, once the flavors have had a chance to meld.

> 15 to 30 razor clams, with liquid reserved, necks and diggers separated (see note)
> 6 to 8 diced medium to large skin-on russet potatoes, half in ¼- to ½-inch cubes, half in ¾- to 1-inch cubes
> Bottled clam juice, as needed, to bring the total volume of clam juice to 4 cups (clams if frozen in water will provide a substantial amount of liquid), plus more as needed
> 2 to 3 slices thick-cut bacon, cooked and crumbled
> 6 tablespoons unsalted butter, plus more as needed
> ½ large yellow onion, diced
> 1 stalk celery, diced (optional)
> 1 carrot, finely diced (optional)
> 1 to 3 cloves garlic, minced (optional)
> ½ teaspoon HonDashi (Japanese fish soup stock in granule form)
> 2 cups half-and-half, plus more as needed
> ½ teaspoon Worcestershire sauce
> ½ teaspoon Tabasco sauce, or to taste
> Several leaves of fresh basil, chopped, or 1 to 2 teaspoons dried basil, to taste
> 1 teaspoon freshly ground black pepper, or to taste
> 1 teaspoon kosher or sea salt, or to taste

If the clam necks are not already ground, grind or finely chop and place them, with their liquid, into a large bowl. Chop the clam bodies into ¼- to ½-inch pieces on a small cutting board placed into a shallow baking pan; this will allow you to more easily reserve the juice. Add the chopped clams with their juices to the bowl and place in the refrigerator.

Place the potatoes into a 6- to 8-quart heavy pot. Cover with the reserved clam liquid (from both fresh and defrosted clams), bottled clam juice as needed to make 4 cups, and enough cold water to cover the potatoes by 2½ to 3 inches. Bring to a boil, cover, and reduce the heat to medium-high. Simmer, stirring occasionally, until the large potato chunks are just tender in the center, about 15 to 25 minutes.

Meanwhile, in a large skillet, fry the bacon over medium-high heat until crisp. Remove the bacon and all but 2 tablespoons bacon fat. Add 1 tablespoon of the butter to the skillet. Add the onion, celery, and carrot and sauté for 5 minutes over medium-low heat, until the vegetables are softened. Add the garlic and sauté another minute. Remove from the heat. Crumble the bacon and add to the skillet.

When the potatoes are cooked, reduce the heat to low. Stir in the clam necks, sautéed vegetables, HonDashi, half-and-half, Worcestershire, Tabasco, basil, remaining 5 tablespoons butter, pepper, and salt.

Bring the mixture to a low simmer. Add the chopped clam bodies, stir, and simmer for about 2 minutes, or until just cooked through. Add more half-and-half, butter, or clam juice, if desired, and adjust seasoning. Serve with a dollop of butter (optional) and a few grinds of black pepper.

Note: Clams may be fresh, frozen, or a combination of both—Lee's usual choice. He likes to use a preponderance of necks, often from the freezer, saving the diggers for frying or other preparation.

CHAPTER 8

LICENSED TO CARRY

It was just happenstance that I started digging with a shovel, but I've stayed with it. In fact, I use the same shovel I bought at a garage sale decades ago, the one I used to dig my first clam. I sometimes call it a clam gun, a term that dates to the earliest days of razor clam digging. "Clam gun" pretty much surprises people the first time they hear it. Who digs clams with a gun?

The locution is always good for a joke. You don't need to load the gun to hunt razor clams, or get a license from the Bureau of Alcohol, Tobacco, and Razor Clams. Back in the day, I don't think folks chuckled much over the expression, or if they did maybe the chuckles came from a particular kind of intimacy, the way a pioneer might have called an ax Ol' Betsy. Clam guns were part of livelihood and survival, a way to dig clams fast and effectively. These days people still use the term, if more self-consciously because of sensitivities about guns, and some still say they're going to go shoot some clams. Nevertheless, I was startled to hear many people calling the *tube* a clam gun. I'd always understood the shovel to be the gun. Razor clamming has limited slang, and "clam gun" is the preeminent contribution. So, who owned the right to keep and bear arms, and swagger down the beach?

A Tube Digger preparing to hoist

To describe the contenders: Those Who Dig With A Shovel use a special shovel with a narrow blade and either a long or short shaft. They prospect for clams by banging the shovel against the beach like Neanderthals. After spotting a show, they drop to one knee as if proposing marriage and excavate with a fast, hoe-like motion. Then they reach in with bare hands and get the clam, or, if it's deep, they scoop like a human backhoe. Typically, Shovelers dig in the surf zone, where the water washes in and the sand is softer, and the clams can dig down fast. They wear waders or hip boots. Digging feels like sport. It takes some time to master the shovel, but it can be quick and has always been the preferred method for commercial diggers.

Those Who Dig With A Tube use a tube, in varying lengths and diameters, made of plastic or metal. Tubers tend to dig in the upper sand, which is drier. They spot a show—sometimes a hole, but often just a slight dimple—and stand behind the show on the beach side, looking toward the water. Then they wiggle, rock, or twist the tube into the sand, put a finger over the vent hole, and perform the stoop-and-hoist. They lift up and uncover the vent, and out drops the coring. If no clam comes out, they dig again in the same hole, sometimes two or three times, going deeper each time. The clams are

A Shoveler demonstrating classic form and tenacity

essentially immobile because the upper sand is dense and comparatively dry. Tubers don't have to contend with waves or get wet, and in reasonable weather they can get away with sneakers and shorts.

Two different philosophies. Both are called digging, but they are different forms of excavation. There are hybrid strategies—Tubers will dig in the surf, and Shovelers will look for dimples in drier sand—but folks tend to prefer one style or the other.

Those Who Dig With A Tube appear to be the distinct majority.

"That's a clam *gun*, right?" I said to the clerk, pointing to a clamming shovel.

"No, that's a clam *shovel*," he said. I thought he must have misunderstood me. I was at the Dennis Company's display of clamming gear at the Ocean Shores Razor Clam Festival.

"What's this?" I said, pointing to a metal tube, standing upright on the floor and in formation with a dozen others, admittedly like a soldier on parade.

"That's a clam gun."

The clerk proclaiming this disturbing intelligence turned out to be Randy Dennis, co-owner of the Dennis Company, which was founded by his great-grandfather more than a hundred years ago. Dennis was an experienced razor clammer and a seller of clam gear. He was one of the prime movers in bringing back the Long Beach Razor Clam Festival. He started digging with his dad as a toddler. His wife's family were also dedicated clammers. In short, he was as bona fide an expert as I was likely to find. And he was calling the shovel a shovel and the tube . . . a gun.

I told him I had a razor clam shovel, an old thing I bought at a garage sale decades ago, and I had always understood it was a clam gun. No, Dennis assured me, what I had was a *shovel*.

Having heard I had an older shovel, the other clerk leaped in. Razor clammers never miss an opportunity to discuss the finer points of gear. "Is it a True Temper? True Temper made the best shovels, but they stopped making them decades ago. The market was too specialized, too small."

I said I didn't know what brand it was, but it was pretty old.

He said it could be a True Temper. "They are classics, collector's items. People go to the dump looking for old ones to refurbish."

Meanwhile, a mother and her son, no taller than a hip wader, arrived. "Oh, my son loves to clam," said the mom. "We clam all the time."

"We have tubes that are cut down to fit him," said Dennis, going back to his customers. I was wondering if the humble clam gun—er, shovel—in my storage area was in fact a collectible True Temper. Hmmm, that would be a happy thing. But mostly I felt a pit in my stomach. How could I have been so mistaken about the clam gun?

I had to ask Dennis again.

"This is a shovel," Dennis said with authority, shaking a shovel. "And this is the *clam gun*," he said, pointing to a tube.

"He calls the clam shovel . . . a shovel!" I said to Karen. "Could the tube really be a clam gun? Am I losing my mind?"

We walked into the main convention hall of the festival. Purveyors of clam chowders competing for blue ribbons were all around, filling the room with a dense, cream-rich fog.

"Didn't the shovel used to be called the clam gun?" I asked, gasping for oxygen.

"Let it go," she said.

"But don't you remember, when I first started clamming, and I called it a gun?"

"Yes."

"This is really strange."

"Why don't we get some chowder," she said, gripping me tightly and handing me a little plastic tasting spoon.

A few weeks later I went to Washington's other razor clam festival at Long Beach and resumed my inquiries. I spoke with Bob Andrew, the mayor of Long Beach, at his bakery, before he dedicated the newly spurting razor clam sculpture. Andrew had grown up razor clamming just like Randy Dennis, and he confirmed what Dennis had told me: that the shovel was the shovel and the tube was a gun. My cinnamon roll stuck in my throat.

"I like the shovel," Andrew said. "You have to dig a special way with the shovel. But the clam gun has taken over. Shovel is old world. The new world is the tube. The majority of the people who use the shovel, they break the shell. They can't get the concept of using the shovel."

In contradiction to Mayor Andrew and Randy Dennis, a few folks I canvassed that day said the shovel was the gun. Others lowered their eyes and walked away quickly. Some topics are best avoided unless you like a bar fight.

Of course, this discussion begged the question of why any implement for digging razor clams would be called a "gun." A shovel doesn't shoot anything, nor does a tube. So, what gives? I had my theories. I thought you could argue that the shovel looks like a gun in profile, but figured the term's appropriateness most likely resided in its employ—a special device used in a special way against a targeted quarry. Take aim, fire, and get your man, the clam.

As far as the tube being a gun, my friend Jared Smith espoused a widely shared theory. "The tube is like the barrel of a gun," he said. "So the clam tube is the gun." Jared had built a clam tube in his seventh-grade shop class in Seattle in the 1960s, bending sheet metal to make the tube and soldering on a cap. "We called it a clam gun," he said. Older kids were making roach clips.

The puzzle of the "clam gun" gnawed at me, so I dug around in the old accounts of razor clamming. Peter F. Halferty, the canned razor clam impresario and entrepreneur, once again talked to me from the past. He wrote in 1919 that, when the tide goes out, razor clams "draw in their necks, leaving a hole in the sand about the size of a lead pencil which is a good mark for *the clam digger's gun, a narrow bladed shovel with a handle about two feet long*" (my emphasis).

Ha! That was unambiguous. The shovel was originally a gun. Despite what Andrew the mayor of Long Beach had said, and despite what Dennis the seller of razor clam gear had told me. There is nary a mention of the clam tube in Halferty's account, which was not surprising since, as I slowly came to realize, the tube had yet to be invented.

Halferty continued, "If a clam digger fails to get him 'the first shot' he will be safe in 'The Trenches' during that tide." Halferty was not afraid to be influenced by World War I and extend the gun metaphor, even though the Great War had ended only a year earlier, in 1918.

Norah Berg, in her memoir *Lady on the Beach*, confirmed what Halferty had penned. She wrote, "A clam gun is a shovel with sharp edges, a long blade, and, usually, a short handle. . . . [When the commercial season opened] every man, woman and child had strapped

A cartoon from the era before tubes were invented. The term "clam gun" enticed and confused neophytes, and continues to do so. Courtesy Gene Woodwick/Coastal Heritage Services

on a clam belt and was carrying his own clam gun and surf sack."

The clam shovel, again, is unequivocally a clam gun.

But around the 1960s the story changes. Rules for razor clamming suddenly included the tube in the list of permitted digging tools, for example.

So, as Seattle was on the verge of its 1962 World's Fair, another, equally important watershed event had occurred: the clam tube had been invented and had come into common use. And these tube devices came to be called guns—as, for example, in a newspaper story titled "A Lousy Weekend to be a Clam," which reminded clammers that only morning digging was allowed and they had to "put away their guns and shovels at noon."

I asked everybody how the tube originated, but nobody had any idea. I thought maybe it could have been patented, so I called the patent office in Washington, D.C.

"Patents before 1976 are not searchable by key words," said the woman's voice. "Do you know the patent number?"

"No."

"Do you know the inventor?"

"No."

"Then you'll have to search by sub-classification at a U.S. patent office," she concluded triumphantly.

I hung up the phone, discouraged. It sounded like looking for a needle in a haystack of a million patents. But just for grins I did an online search using keywords, and lo and behold, within short order up popped the original patent for a tubular "clam digging device," dated August 13, 1957. Filed by James E. Batstone of Shelton, Washington. I danced with joy around the house.

Later, I made contact with Batstone's children. Their dad was proud of his invention, they said, but he never made much money off of it. For a living he drove logging trucks and worked in the mills early in his career; it was unsteady employment and he supplemented his income by working as an electrician's helper and doing other odd jobs. He was a carpenter and all-around can-do guy who, for a hobby, liked to restore small vintage engines and rebuild antique clocks. He loved figuring out how to get things working. How he came to be inspired to invent the tube is unknown, but he was a frequent razor clammer and unhappy that for so many the shovel was difficult to use and resulted in breakage of the clam's fragile shell.

Batstone created the tube at age thirty-eight in his home workshop. His invention looks nearly identical to the clam tubes in use today, a stovepipe-like cylinder sealed at one end, with a crosspiece handle and finger-controlled "air trapping and releasing vent." Batstone's vent was a small copper nipple that he braised onto the tube; it extended upward. The device relies on a vacuum principle known to every child—the one that enables you to lift milk from a glass in a straw and then drop it onto the table, by putting your finger over the top of the straw and then taking your finger off.

Batstone retailed his invention as "The Sandpiper, the clam digger's sweetheart." According to his patent application, his objective was "to devise and provide a simple, practical and economical device."

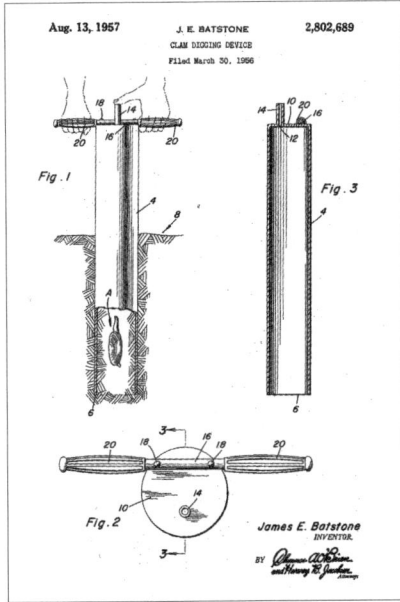

James Batstone transformed razor clamming with his patented razor clamming tube invention of 1957. When lifting a core of sand from the beach, the operator placed a finger over the vent (no. 14), then removed the finger to release the partial vacuum, letting the core of sand drop. The tube was effective, and learning to use it was comparatively easy. Nowadays the majority of razor clam diggers employ some version of Batstone's tube. Courtesy US Patent Office

In fact, his invention transformed razor clam digging. Tubes were easy to learn to use, allowed the operator to stay dry, and mangled far fewer clams compared to inexperienced shovel diggers. They effectively dug in the hard sand of the upper beach while the immobilized clam waited for the return of the tide. They were revolutionary and immediately accepted. The Clan of Tubers was born.

Batstone soon had a flood of orders; he envisioned a weekly output of up to five hundred, according to a newspaper story, and he sold the device himself and through area sporting goods stores. However, his fellow citizens quickly stole his idea and began making imitations.

Presumably, stores, merchants, and others marketed the tube as a clam gun to drive sales, taking advantage of that existing term. It may have felt natural to call any razor clam–digging implement a clam gun. However it happened, the tube staked out a claim for itself as the clam gun almost immediately after Batstone received his patent in 1957, and it has gained ground ever since.

James Batstone in 1971, some fourteen years after he invented the razor clam tube. Courtesy Betsy Batstone-Cunningham and the Batstone family

Despite the competition, Batstone himself regularly bought galvanized stovepipe and fabricated clam tubes for sale, loading up the kids and driving to the beach in his Ford station wagon to retail them by the roadside, as entrepreneurs still occasionally do today with their own versions. He was offered $3,000 for the clam tube patent, according to family lore, but turned it down. However, all the copycats and near-copyright infringers undercut what could have been a tidy business. Batstone wasn't a marketer by nature, and he didn't have the means to go after imitators. Though he apparently never made a lot of money from his brainstorm, he and his wife traveled to China in 1982 after it opened to the West following President Nixon's historic 1972 trip, and he told friends and his fellow travelers he was using the dollars he earned from "inventing the clam gun." How much that was wishful thinking and how much a good story is unclear. For the last twenty years of his career, he drove a truck for the Mason County power utility, and he passed away in 1996.

There were two significant improvements made on the basic tube in the years following its invention. In 1963, John Puckett of Olympia, Washington, patented a short tube connected by a hollow shaft to a *T*-shaped handle with the vent hole underneath one side of the handle. The ergonomic vent-hole location made the digging process much easier, and that improvement has become the standard.

The second innovation came in 1979. Walter M. Madsen of Madras, Oregon, added piping inside the length of the main tube in order to release the partial vacuum that forms in the hole as you hoist the coring. It's that vacuum that makes lifting so difficult. If you see emergency vehicles at the beach, it's as likely as not that they are there for somebody slumped over a tube. Madsen's tube actually had a moving part, a plug over the piping opening. When the digger pushed downward, the plug kept the piping from being blocked with sand. On the upward pull the plug slid down, allowing air to enter and releasing or at least reducing the suction.

Tubes vented in this way, with or without moving parts, never really caught on. But around 2013 a Cadillac version of the vented tube hit the shelves. Instead of a venting pipe within the tube, it had a shallow *V*-shaped piece of metal attached to the outside. Many were claiming that it worked great, and stainless steel models were flying out of the Dennis Company's store in Long Beach even though they cost more than $100. "We started selling them three days ago and it created a sensation," said Randy Dennis, who said his dad had used one and thought it reduced digging effort by almost 25 percent.

I couldn't wait to try one out and was initially excited. The tube glided in and out of the sand as if it were greased. But subsequent pulls seemed harder. Perhaps the *V*-shaped slot had clogged with sand. And it was heavy to drag around the beach. Even worse, who would risk denting such an expensive tool to prospect and bang? As it happens, for just this reason, the Dennis Company was also selling a "thumper." Tall as a person, and with a metal weight at one end, the staff did a great job of banging the beach and scaring the bejabbers out of clams. I saw some people on the beach with these setups—heavy tube in one hand and thumper tied to their waists dragged behind them. They looked like Marley's ghost, encumbered and condemned to wander. Nonetheless, the tube is a well-crafted item and made in America. At any rate, stainless steel has less friction pushing through the sand than aluminum, and much less than PVC.

Shovels have seen little innovation along the lines that clam tubes have enjoyed. Indeed, shovels have been devolving. Tool steel isn't what it used to be, and the few patent applications for improved clam shovels are gimmicky. The earliest clam shovels were made by scrappy individuals who reshaped standard shovels and spades to their liking. True Temper, maker of the "collectible" razor clam shovels, started making clam shovels in the 1930s after it merged with a number of other small companies to became the largest hand tool manufacturer in America. Commercial availability from True Temper didn't stop folks from customizing, though. "Clam guns are manufactured in a subtle variety of sizes and shapes, all of them wrong," wrote *Seattle Times* reporter Byron Fish in 1952. "(An experienced digger) wants a different crook in the neck, or a longer handle or a shorter handle, or the blade doesn't suit him. All clam fans must tamper with the manufacturer's version."

True Temper made razor clam shovels for fifty years, then stopped in the 1980s. Commercial razor clam canning had by that time mostly disappeared, and it was not worthwhile making specialized shovels for regional recreational markets. Besides, in 1984 and '85, Washington's clamming season was canceled due to NIX, and thus a major market was entirely gone.

Clamming shovels are still available today in many different shapes and sizes, many made by local suppliers who use plasma cutters to shape off-the-shelf garden shovels into a narrow blade. They work fine but are not the heavy-duty razor clamming shovels of old, which were made of forged "special analysis steel," as the 1971 True Temper wholesale catalog put it, with one-piece construction and a variety of neck angles to choose from.

No wonder the old True Temper clam shovels are prized.

Clam Guns Come In Many Shapes and Sizes But All Have Faults

Razor clammers looking for the right shovel are as picky as baseball players looking for the right bat, according to this newspaper story that ran on March 9, 1952, five years before razor clamming tubes appeared on the scene. Drawing by Al Pratt/*The Seattle Times*. Copyright 1952 Seattle Times Company, used with permission

Now, there's a curious thing here, which is the description of how accomplished diggers used the clam shovel in the early years. Diggers today, and for many decades, typically make one or two or three quick hoe-like excavations about six inches on the seaward side of the show, inching toward and sometimes slightly underneath the clam, then reaching down and getting the clam. If you are skillful or fortunate, it's a quick process, and you grab the exposed hinge side of the clam. If you are not so skillful, you end up on your knees, digging in the sand with your hands while the surf crashes around your shoulders.

But this is not precisely how the expert shovel clammers of yore did it, at least judging from descriptions like this one, of clammers who "scoop the clam out in a single motion, pop it into the sack and go on tapping without ever straightening up." These diggers scooping out the clam "in a single motion" often used a customized clam shovel with a long, curved blade and a secondary curve at the end, allowing them to get into the sand and under the clam in one smooth effort. The shape of this blade, something like a jai alai scoop, was called a "Westport bend" or "Westport hook." I can well imagine why such a shovel would be called a gun: one shot and the clam was done for. The most famous maker, and presumably the inventor, of the Westport hook was Jack Rhodes. He cut them down from a #2 Fox brand shovel. He numbered each of his shovels, stamping them in the metal along the shaft, and sold them for $10, compared to the $1.50 that other commercial ones went for. Rhodes

Two razor clam shovels in profile. The longer blade on top has a "Westport bend." Shovels courtesy of the Museum of the North Beach collection

or somebody named the implement the Westport hook shovel for its resemblance to the spit in the boat basin at Westport, Washington. The spit later disappeared when the Army Corps of Engineers built a jetty and groins.

Despite the predominance of tubes on the beach today, there are also still plenty of shovels. If you want to chase clams in the surf or wrestle with them mano a mano, the shovel is the way to go. The shovel is sporting and has macho appeal. People concerned with speed and quantity, like commercial diggers, also use shovels. And for many people using a shovel is easier than using a tube, whose hoisting motion has all the pleasure of lifting a stump. The Clan of Shovelers remains strong.

In 2014, I was taking pictures of clams when an older gentleman came up from the surf with a shovel and netful of clams. He was in shirt-sleeves and wearing a beat-up fisherman's hat.

"Whatchya studying?" he asked.

His voice was as gentle as the shallow water rippling around our feet. The beach was mostly empty, and we stood on the wet, reflective sand.

"Just trying to take a picture of the clam digging down," I said.

"You from around here?"

"No, Seattle."

I noticed his shovel blade was mottled, pretty flat and with a pronounced crook in the neck. It looked serious. "Is that a True Temper shovel?" I whispered.

"Yes," he said.

The shovel was pristine. The edges glinted in the light. I might as well have been looking at mithril. I admired it, slack-jawed. He told me he was seventy-six years old, that he had had the shovel since he was twelve, and that as soon as he gets home, he wipes it down and puts it in a bucket of oil.

"As a kid we would once in a while even commercial dig, you could buy a special license and commercially dig," he said. "There wasn't near as many people as now, not near. I've come down the beach for an early night dig, and seen all the lights. I tell my grandkids, I've never seen anything like this, and I've dug clams all my life. It's just change of times, you know. Well, good luck."

And he wandered on up the beach toward his car. He didn't seem to resent the multitude of people that were showing up. I guess as long as there's plenty for all. Here was a guy who came forty-five minutes after the low and got his limit without hurry, with a True Temper shovel. Razor clam royalty.

Language is unpredictable, in constant motion like the ocean itself. There is no absolute right or wrong.

The clam gun started out, as Halferty wrote in 1919, as a narrow-bladed shovel. Then, in 1957, the tube was invented. Very quickly a linguistic jujitsu took place, and the clam tube first shared and then started to take the title of clam gun, which it has now claimed.

Purists, old-timers, and history buffs howl, but in vain. In 2001, *Seattle Post-Intelligencer* outdoor writer Greg Johnston pleaded on behalf of the clam shovel as the gun: "Because the tubes have a barrel like a gun and the shovels look nothing like a gun, most people call the tube a clam gun. But listen: THE TUBE IS NOT A CLAM GUN." But his capital-letter cri de coeur was nothing but a death rattle. The jujitsu move had been completed. Nowadays, even people like Randy Dennis and Mayor Bob Andrew say the tube is the clam gun, truthiness becoming truth, even as they use and prefer the shovel.

State fisheries websites carefully avoid this linguistic quicksand, calling the shovel a shovel and the tube a tube. Very accurate, very prosaic. No guns.

"Clam gun" is an epithet from a bygone era, and every activity loves its lingo. Razor clamming is a real hunt with a hidden quarry and the excitement of the catch. "Clam gun" captures that. A bit tongue-in-cheek today, perhaps, but still. For me, the clam shovel is the gun. That's the history. The shovel's simplicity, in partnership with the sense of sport, give it primacy. I'll use a tube and even feel the temptation to call it a gun; there is that much social pressure. But I resist. I'm waging a rearguard action, even with myself, but I'm sticking to my guns. And if you want to fight about it, you can find me down in the surf.

BROCK'S RAZOR CLAMS WITH BLACK BEAN SAUCE
Makes 4 servings

Brock Johnson is head chef at the Dahlia Lounge, one of restauranteur Tom Douglas's signature establishments in Seattle. Johnson occasionally razor clammed as a youth in Oregon, but the activity was a much bigger deal for his grandfather, who grew up on the Shoalwater Reservation, and his dad.

Johnson came to razor clams through the culinary world, not via his tribal heritage. Chefs these days are expected to "walk the walk," he says, and participate in every aspect of food culture. "They forage for mushrooms, catch fish—especially here in the Northwest—and get hands dirty gardening."

And go razor clamming, naturally enough.

When I asked Johnson if he razor clammed using the shovel or the tube, he laughed. "I'm not good enough to use the shovel. I think the tube is cheating, but a couple of days empty handed and it's pretty easy to put down the shovel."

Johnson's dish uses fermented black beans and is inspired by classic Chinese dishes such as geoduck clam with black bean sauce. The combination of fermented beans and chicken stock is a staple at the Dahlia Lounge, used for their stir-fries.

This recipe calls for asparagus, but Johnson suggests using whatever vegetable is in season: asparagus in spring, green beans in summer, and broccoli in fall.

When Johnson couldn't find fresh razor clams recently he ended up buying some that were frozen whole in the shell. He found, to his surprise, that the meat from these was "far superior—very delicious—without a doubt better" than frozen meat that was already cleaned and ready to go. Whole frozen clams are not generally available to either consumers or restaurateurs, but such storage is something the recreational digger might consider, though it is space demanding in the freezer.

Fermented black beans are available in most Asian groceries or ethnic food sections of grocery stores, as is sambal, a spicy Southeast Asian condiment made of chiles and small amounts of other ingredients. But other hot sauces will do as well.

FOR THE BLACK BEAN STIR-FRY SAUCE

½ cup soy sauce

3 tablespoons sugar

1 cup chicken stock

1 tablespoon sambal (or other hot sauce)

1½ tablespoons fermented black beans, chopped

1 tablespoon cornstarch

1 teaspoon sesame oil

FOR THE RAZOR CLAMS

4 tablespoons vegetable oil

1 tablespoon minced ginger

1 tablespoon minced garlic

1 tablespoon minced scallions

1 medium yellow onion, sliced

4 cups shiitake mushrooms, stemmed and sliced

1 pound asparagus, cut into 1-inch lengths

2 cups razor clam meat, cut into ½-inch-wide strips across the length of the clam (if there is lots of spawn, scrape some out)

Steamed rice, for serving

To make the black bean stir-fry sauce

Mix the soy sauce, sugar, chicken stock, sambal, fermented black beans, cornstarch, and sesame oil. Set aside.

To prepare the razor clams

Place a wok or large skillet over medium-high heat. Add the oil and then the ginger, garlic, and scallions. Cook for 30 seconds and then add the onion and mushrooms and stir-fry for 1 minute. Add the asparagus and continue to cook until the vegetables are lightly softened, about 30 seconds longer. Add the reserved black bean stir-fry sauce and bring to a boil to thicken the sauce. Finally, add the clams, and stir to combine. The clams cook quickly and will pretty much poach in the sauce right when they are stirred in. Remove the pan from the heat and serve with rice.

CHAPTER 9

EATING THEM, AFTER ALL, IS THE POINT

> Oh! sweet friends, hearken to me. [The chowder] was made of small juicy clams, scarcely bigger than hazel nuts, mixed with pounded ship biscuits, and salted pork cut up into little flakes! the whole enriched with butter, and plentifully seasoned with pepper and salt.
> —HERMAN MELVILLE, *Moby-Dick*

THE question of what to do with your mess of razor clams is not a difficult one. Clammers are creatures of habit. We have our rituals and family recipes. Even before stepping out the door for the day's hunt, we pretty much know how we are going to prepare the catch, if fortunate enough to get a good haul. Just thinking about that distinctive razor clam flavor makes our mouths water.

The clam itself is large and meaty, without a bone in its body. It doesn't have to be purged of sand and grit like hard-shell clams. It doesn't have to be blanched and peeled like the giant geoduck clam. It's a cooperative foodstuff. Just separate the clam from the shell by cutting the adductor muscles or dipping it in boiling water, remove the gills and stomach, slice the clam in half with knife or scissors,

Salt and pepper shakers in the shape of razor clams

and rinse with water. A fat six-inch razor clam in the shell weighs out at six or seven ounces, a real heft in the hand. It takes just a couple of minutes to dress one, and you end up with about three ounces of beautiful, ivory-colored meat. Even if you overcook it into chewing gum, it's razor clam–flavored gum, and that distinctive sweet taste makes all the jaw work worthwhile.

Grizzly bears in Alaska eat Pacific razor clams, which must count as some kind of endorsement. They wander down to ocean beaches at low tide and dig with big paws, excavating the buried treasure and devouring it in under a minute. Who can blame the bears for their efforts, even if the clams are available to them only a few hours a day during low tides? The clams are full of "digestible energy," as the biologists put it. In the human world they are known as "premier table fare."

Gene Woodwick, now a book author and coastal historian, was nineteen years old when she started cooking for loggers in western Washington in the early 1960s. The men rose before dawn, and, if the job site was near the ocean and the tides cooperated, they would go to the shore and gather razor clams at lunchtime. Back at camp they would hand her the clam meat. Woodwick had no idea what to do with it. She was from landlocked Colorado and unfamiliar with seafood. But they told her: dip in buttermilk, roll in bread crumbs, and fry. So she made a fine coating from the bread that she baked daily and fried the clams up in butter. Some of the loggers preferred them cooked with no breading, and "just barely warmed." Either way, they packed them away as a special treat.

For my part, the meal starts while cleaning the clam. I didn't put raw morsels of clam into my mouth at first. But ultimately, curiosity and pleasure at the sushi restaurant led me to eat pieces of the clam as I was cleaning it. I would have to describe that as a revelation. It gave me an appreciation for the varied parts of the clam, and for how better to cook it, or not overcook it.

The first treat is always the adductor muscle, which is basically like a scallop—just smaller—and every clam has two. Sometimes it sticks to the clam shell and I just scrape it off and pop into my mouth. A nice morsel to keep me going while cleaning a full limit, and sometimes Karen's limit as well. Another treat is the neck, which people normally think of as tough, to be ground up for chowder, an afterthought to the fried digger. But raw it is crunchy, like a blanched slice of carrot. Not at all something to be relegated to second tier. The foot, or digger—the bulk of the clam—is soft and chewy, and, in season, filled with spawn, sometimes referred to as butter. It can taste mineral-y like some oysters. There is a fourth texture as well, the flesh of the mantle, thin and crisp. So, three ounces of boneless protein provide a symphony of textures, each with a counterpoint of sweetness. We are not a food culture that places a premium on texture, which is a shame. The fresh-from-the-sand razor clam contains all these textures in one tidy package. There is a culinary journey to be had there.

Razor clams are rarely seen on menus or seafood counters, even in the sushi-crazed, locally sourced–loving Northwest. This is a stunning oversight, though there are some practical reasons. Razor clams are a wild foodstuff that must be hunted and gathered—not farmed like oysters, mussels, hard-shell clams, and geoducks; supplies are thus not entirely reliable. Most of the wild harvest in Washington is reserved for recreational, not commercial, diggers (a happy thing for the average razor clammer). As far as sushi bars, it turns out local sushi fans are not so adventuresome after all, preferring the meat-like textures of tuna and hamachi to crunch; demand is low, making purchase by restaurateurs tricky.

It's also true that razor clams have slipped from public consciousness. If people were more familiar with this bounty, perhaps interest and demand would grow. But as it is, most clams harvested commercially end up as crab bait, just as the Razor Clam Canners Association deplored in its letter to housewives more than half a century ago. The reason is still the same: razor clams are a quality bait for a high-ticket item. "Razor clams are what ocean crabs want for dinner," says Dale Beasley, the president of the Columbia River Crab Fishing Association. So desirable are the clams to the crabs that just half a clam can suffice for attracting them. And razor clams will last four or five days soaking in the trap, whereas squid, another popular bait, rots in just a day or so.

In recent banner razor clam years, the Quinault Indian Nation has commercially dug a remarkable 800,000 pounds annually, and nearly all of that has gone for crab bait, according to Alan Heather, manager of the fish house, as everyone calls the Quinault Pride Seafood enterprise. The bulk of the poundage comes in the spring when the clams are largest and digging is during daylight hours. Mostly the tribe sells to large crab-bait wholesalers. With tons of freshly dug clams delivered by the truckload, and other seafood such as salmon to process, it's often impossible to do much more than sell the bounty quickly and keep the cash flow in balance.

The fish house shucks and cleans a small percentage according to the strict handling regulations required for human consumption, then sends the meat to local markets. "We've tried to move product back East," says Heather. "They just shake their heads. They don't

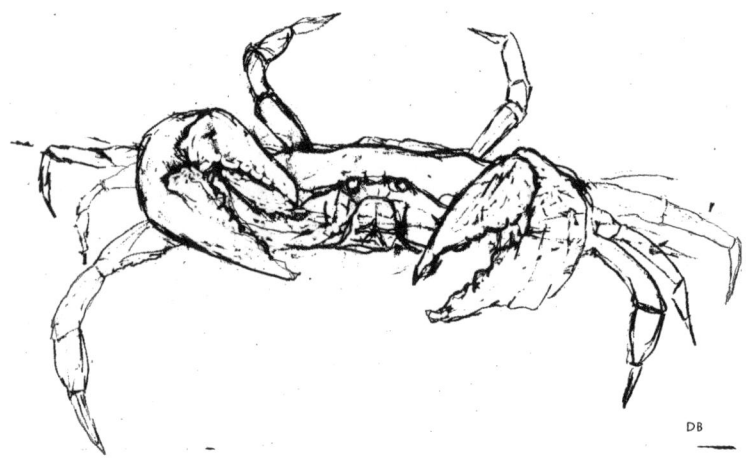

Coastal Dungeness crabs love to eat razor clams. The majority of razor clams harvested commercially goes for use as crab bait.

know what to do with it. Even though we've sent people back to show them. But to break in is very difficult."

A few clams are kept in the shell, inspected for cracks, matched for size, wrapped with a rubber band (to keep the shell closed and the clam fresher), and shipped live on gel ice to Asian markets in Vancouver, British Columbia. Attempts to sell in Japan or China, and copy the lucrative commercial success of geoducks, have failed. One problem is the clams themselves. At least with current methods, they are hard to keep alive during plane flights, according to Heather, and Asian markets require a living product.

The uncertainty of harvest, underdeveloped fresh markets even in the Northwest, and steady demand from crabbers all conspire to keep razor clams out of the culinary limelight. If you do happen to see them fresh or frozen at a fish counter, they can sell for a discouraging $17 a pound, and they just don't taste as good as the freshly dug ones. Some Costco stores occasionally have them for about $11 a pound, harvested and packaged in Alaska. A handful of specialty shops on the coast buy, process, and can razor clams, echoing an industry that once thrived.

In 2013 the Quinault Indian Nation's razor clams received the "Best Choice" designation from the Monterey Bay Aquarium Seafood Watch. This is the program's coveted highest rating for human-consumed seafood and recognizes sustainability of harvest, good management, and lack of by-catch and environmental harm. "We've got a great product here and want people to know about it," says Scott Mazzone, the tribal shellfish biologist. At the moment, though, most of the locally sourced, sustainably harvested seafood delicacy goes right into the blast freezer and twenty-pound containers, and ultimately into the crabber's bait box. Razor clams could be a triumphant Northwest foodstuff, but they have yet to be given the full star makeover. If you want to fully enjoy razor clams, you have to do like the bears: head to the beach at low tide and dig them yourself.

I visited with chef Taichi Katamura at his Japanese restaurant Sushi Kappo Tamura in Seattle to get his take on razor clams. Katamura's philosophy is to celebrate local ingredients in the Japanese style. When he emigrated from Japan, he specifically came to Washington because of the smorgasbord of seafood, mushrooms, and other fare right in the backyard.

But razor clams are not one of the more popular or promoted items in his restaurant. Partially that's because clams in the shell are hard to find, and that's the only way he'll buy them, to accurately assess freshness; he won't buy shucked razor clams. He also says that it's hard to figure out how much he should buy, if any, even when he can find razor clams in the shell. Scallops and surf clam, farm raised in Japan, are on the menu year-round, and they satisfy

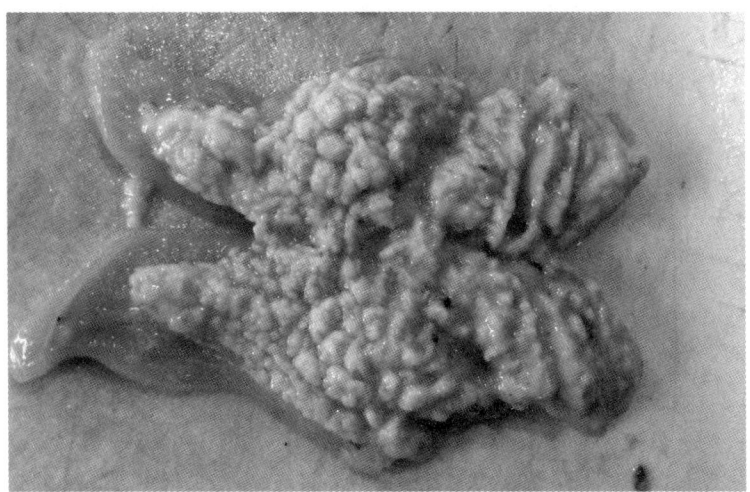

A razor clam's foot, butterflied open for cleaning and cooking, reveals the spawn inside.

the limited mollusk demand, along with the local geoduck. Buying razors is risky, even though they are inexpensive compared with geoduck.

I asked Katamura if he prefers the razor clam raw or cooked. He says he prefers raw, hands down. He likes the crunch. He said that Japanese, and Asians in general, appreciate every texture. "Crunch means fresh to Asian people," he said. "In America crunch is OK for chips, but not for seafood."

I asked him which part of the clam he serves to customers, the neck or the digger, if someone happens to order razor clam sushi in a moment of curiosity about local seafood. He paused. "They don't know the difference," he said. I was a little shocked, as someone who ate a digger would have a completely different experience from someone who ate the neck. They would hardly realize it was from the same animal. He said that for people who don't know the clam, he typically gives them the soft digger, but he serves both the crunchier neck and the digger, not wasting any part of the shucked clam.

Katamura cleaned the clams I'd brought with a sharp knife and put them in iced salt water, where he said they'd keep for up to three

A plate of razor clam sushi

days. Then he made us several pieces of sushi, fishing out the clam pieces with chopsticks. (When I tried to help and reached in for a piece, he tsked, "I never put my fingers in the water.") He first cut up the neck, creating four equal-sized rectangles. He then knifed little cuts halfway through each piece. He said the clam neck is too slick to absorb soy sauce, and such cuts give the salty liquid a place to cling. I also thought it would make the clam easier to eat—not exactly tenderizing it, but making it easier to chew and bite into smaller pieces should you so desire.

He draped these morsels over sushi rice, then turned to the digger, cutting it in half lengthwise and scraping off most of the big mound of spawn. "You are scraping off the spawn?" I said. "Many people say that's the best part." He looked surprised. But in Katamura's method, scraping off the soft spawn, or most of it, was preferred. He arranged the sushi pieces, neck and digger, on a ceramic plate with a squeeze of lemon. We gobbled them in no time. "Why don't Westerners like the razor clam raw?" I asked.

"It's not in the culture," he said. "For us, it's a crime to bread and fry it. We eat it straight."

But eating raw is an infinitesimal percentage of razor clam consumption, not even a speck in the ocean of chowders and mountains of fried. Those two preparations are the vast preference, in many variations. Fried does a fine job of capturing and holding the razor clam flavor, with coatings of flour or panko bread crumbs, or, for some coastal folks, of crumbled Ritz or Goldfish crackers. Razor clam chowders are tasty, and people in the Northwest are mad for New England–style concoctions of chopped razor clams cooked with onion, potato, and milk or cream. At the Long Beach and Ocean Shores razor clam festivals, crowds throng to the chowder contest, tasting white chowder after white chowder.

A typical New England–style clam chowder recipe calls for bacon, onion, potato, often celery, and hard-shell clams to produce the seafood flavor backbone. Razor clams are a different animal from hard-shell clams. You don't steam razor clams open, and even ground and simmered they don't produce much potent nectar. Yes, you can add bottled clam juice, use liquid from steamed hard-shell clams, or make stock from fish bones, chicken, lobster shells, or dried bonito flakes (as in the Japanese dashi). Many embrace such approaches, though that's not fully exploiting the distinctive razor clam flavor. For that reason, I've always considered making razor clam chowder a challenge. Home cooks who've dug a netful of clams have the luxury of dumping in an extravagance of chopped clam into the hot soup just before serving, to get the most razor clam flavor. Just about any soup recipe benefits from adding more razor clams.

I got a clue for making a razor clammy chowder from a coastal resident. I asked if he liked to dig razor clams and eat them. Affirmative to both, he said, and his family likes chowder.

"How do you make it?"

He said he starts with the usual—some rendered bacon, cooking onions, and potatoes—then adds milk and chicken stock, and, from his larder, canned clams and all the nectar in the cans.

"You can your clams?" I said, my ears perking up. Now, Karen from time to time will make jam or pickles, but canning clams seemed not just retro but positively anachronistic.

"Oh yes," he replied. "You need to pressure cook them. Between me, my wife, and daughter, we bring back forty-five clams, three limits. We eat one mess, can the rest in pint jars, process ninety minutes at eleven pounds." He rattled off the details with the casual authority of someone who's done it innumerable times and knows all the ins and outs.

"A lot of folks in Grays Harbor can clams; it makes a better chowder," he said. "The canning process makes them soft. You can eat them right from the can. You fry them, boil them, they can get tough."

I thought about this for quite a while. I remembered walking past two women in an RV during one of my early razor clamming forays. They were parked by a creek under a shade tree, set up for a weekend of clamming and canning. I checked in with them before I left. We've put up seventy-five jars, they told me. So far.

Now I felt a dawning revelation. I looked back over some of the historical recipes. Many, if not most, called for canned clams with the juice, or the addition of razor clam nectar leftover from the canning process. Rarely fresh clams. For example, in 1937, a prominent Aberdeen restaurateur named Rube Walden submitted a chowder recipe for use at the first annual "clamboree." It called for "diced lean bacon fried brown, flour added to secure a roux, equal parts of clam nectar and fresh milk brought to a boil, braised onions added with potatoes until barely done, then scalded, minced Grays Harbor razor clams. Season with pepper, salt and ground mace, add parsley and garlic."

A riff on the classic recipe, to be sure, but where was this "equal part of nectar" coming from? Looking at vintage razor clam labels reveals that canneries provided not only minced and whole clams, in their liquid, but clam nectar and clam juice as well. Three tablespoons

Canned razor clams and single-serving "clam juice" bottles from the early 1900s, good for whatever ails you. Courtesy Museum of the North Beach

of nectar to a cup of water to make a bouillon, advised the recipe on one label. Some labels and recipes recommended nectar-based teas and thin clam-juice soups for their medicinal properties—"the best thing to take on an empty stomach after a spell of biliousness." Pioneer's Sea Beach Packing offered clam juice in miniature bottles, reputedly popular as chasers in the bar.

In their heyday, canneries steamed or dipped in hot water thousands of clams every day to separate the shell from the clam; that produced something akin to clam stock. Clam shells and scraps would be thrown into the pot as well, according to Lee Marriott, president of the Museum of the North Beach, and the water used again and again, and ultimately reduced to make nectar. The Warrenton cannery extolled its process in an illustrated booklet: "In the packing houses the clams are opened by steam and the delicious pure clam nectar or juice is drawn off to be clarified by a special process which removes all bits of sand or shell, the lingering witnesses to their ocean life. When the clams have been thoroughly cleaned, dressed and packed in their containers, this pure nectar or juice is placed in the can and again surrounds them as it has done in the shell."

Although commercially canned Pacific razor clams have largely disappeared from the marketplace, the home industry of canning razor clams in jars has continued to this day. Consider these entries from a hunting forum I stumbled onto online, in which a fellow posts about canning razor clams with liquid smoke, "turning them into a treat you can break out at camp and share with friends." He advised, "If you don't know how to pressure can, get a book and learn."

Another chimed in: "I have found canning them is by far the best method to store/preserve them. They are sooooo tender."

"How long does a batch last?" asked a commenter.

"You mean in the jar, unopened? Years. Opened around camp? Minutes."

I wondered what it was about home canning that caused the clams to tenderize in this way and produce flavorful razor clam nectar. I could only surmise that the long cooking, while the clams were protected in jars, was responsible, a process not unlike modernist sous vide cooking, which requires special equipment, vacuum packing of ingredients, and cooking at below-boiling temperatures for a very long time. Canning recipes generally call for salt and some lemon juice, and adding salt to the canning liquid was one of Halferty's secrets way back when he launched the commercial canning era near the mouth of the Columbia River, though it didn't stay secret very long.

Sometimes old-school is the best. And if you can do your canning in an RV kitchen by a creek in the shade of tall alder trees, all the better.

I wish I could travel to the coast with my own private sushi chef. I wish we still had the old pressure cooker that took up so much room in the closet gathering dust, which I finally persuaded Karen to part with, and for which she is now saving her best "I told you so."

Norah Berg offered her cooking advice in the course of her book, *Lady on the Beach*. After ten years of experimenting, she wrote, she and her husband liked razor clams best lightly dredged in dry pancake flour, fried to a golden brown, and eaten with coleslaw or green salad. For a special treat, they ground the diggers, cooked them in a white sauce, and served them on toast with a dash of Tabasco. Princely fare, she called it. She also liked them made into patties with an egg, rolled in a flour batter, seasoned with chives or garlic salt, and baked. Razor clams were not quite as tender as butter clams, she said, but they had a much richer flavor.

Because razor clams seldom show up in restaurants, the home cook is at a disadvantage; there is little chance to be inspired by what imaginative chefs might invent. And while razor clam recipes appear in books and web searches, the recipes are typically for the East Coast razor clam, *Ensis directus*, a cousin to *Siliqua patula* but prepared for the table differently and generally cooked in the shell.

It's quite a thought to consider tens of thousands of razor clam diggers all cooking and devouring their catch after the day's harvest. Sometimes, though, Karen and I are too tuckered out from digging and cleaning to eat them the first night. We'll cook them on the next, when we're rested and better able to appreciate their flavor. We reward ourselves that first meal with a surfeit of clams, simply sautéed. No dipping in egg and panko. No stretching out the flavor into potato and milk. No, just a glut of razor clams sautéed in butter and oil. Or maybe, if we're feeling inspired, we'll add a bit of garlic to the oil, or we'll chop and throw in some mushrooms, if they're at hand, or asparagus cut on the diagonal—asparagus is in season in spring, the time when the razor clam spawn is most developed, and makes a welcome contrast in color and taste. Or we'll add some fresh basil as the sautéed clams come off the heat, the green leaves wilting around the hot clams and releasing their fragrance.

But, truthfully, we rarely bother with any of that, though sometimes we'll think about it. Why spend the energy? Why amend the bright, clean flavor of the clams fresh from the sea? That first meal is always just a big panful of clams sautéed with plenty of butter and oil, and a baguette to soak up the wonderful essence.

CHOPPED CLAMS WITH MISO
Makes 4 servings

Chef Taichi Katamura of Sushi Kappo Tamura restaurant in Seattle suggested this dish. Katamura is a fan of eating razor clams raw, and the blanching this recipe calls for is really just the quickest of shocks. Note that he uses clams shucked from the shell without dipping in hot water, which is already a kind of quick blanch.

- **1 cup medium-fine chopped raw clams**
- **¼ cup chopped sweet onion**
- **1 tablespoon white or yellow miso**
- **1 tablespoon sugar**
- **1 teaspoon rice vinegar**
- **1 teaspoon lemon zest (optional)**

Place a medium-sized pot of water over high heat, and bring the water to a simmer. Have ready a large bowl of ice water to put the clams in when they finish cooking. Blanch the clams in the hot water for a short count, about five seconds, then transfer them to the bowl of ice water to stop the cooking. Do the same with the onion. Drain the clams and the onion and add them to a medium-sized bowl. Combine the miso, sugar, and vinegar. Mix a tablespoon of this dressing, or to taste, with the clams. Garnish with the lemon zest. Serve at room temperature or cold.

RAZOR CLAM CEVICHE
Makes 4 appetizer-sized servings

Cold preparations make a nice riposte to fried or sautéed razor clams. Ceviche recipes typically use fish as the main ingredient, "cooking" the protein in lime juice, but razor clams can readily be substituted. Razor clam meat also has a resemblance to conch, and almost any recipe that will work for conch will work for razor clams, summoning visions of the Caribbean.

Ceviche recipes are unlimited in their variations: some use orange or lemon juice in addition to or instead of lime juice; others whir garlic and poblano peppers in a blender together with oil and lime juice; still others add chopped avocado just before serving. The following is a basic ceviche with lime juice, chopped tomato, and cilantro.

- 6 razor clams, chopped medium-fine (about 1¼ cups)
- 1 fresh lime, juiced
- ½ to 1 jalapeño, seeded and finely chopped
- 3 tablespoons minced shallot
- 1 Roma tomato, seeded and finely chopped
- 1 teaspoon olive oil
- ½ teaspoon sugar
- 2½ tablespoons chopped fresh cilantro
- Salt and freshly ground pepper

In a medium-sized bowl, combine the clams, lime juice, and jalapeño (use more or less jalapeño depending on personal preference and the heat of the pepper). Let sit in the refrigerator for 30 minutes to marinate. Add the shallot, tomato, olive oil, sugar, cilantro, and salt and pepper to taste. Let sit in the refrigerator another 30 minutes or so, until the clams are opaque and have reached your desired level of "doneness." Serve in small bowls with cocktail forks.

COCONUT MILK CURRY CLAMS WITH BASIL
Makes 4 servings

Karen devised this Thai-inspired recipe using rich-tasting coconut milk to carry and frame the sweet taste of the clams.

¼ cup water
1½ tablespoons vegetable oil
3 to 4 tablespoons thinly sliced shallots
1 cup chopped asparagus, cut into 2-inch lengths
½ cup thinly sliced red pepper
1 large clove garlic, thinly sliced
4 teaspoons good-quality Thai green chile paste (or to taste)
3 cups roughly chopped razor clams, fresh or previously frozen
¾ cup coconut milk
Fresh lime, for squeezing
Salt and freshly ground black pepper
⅓ cup thinly sliced fresh basil leaves

Steamed rice, for serving

Add the water, oil, shallots, and asparagus to a large sauté pan and place over high heat. Cook until the water has mostly evaporated and the asparagus is al dente, several minutes. Add the red pepper and garlic, and cook until just soft, about 2 more minutes. Work in the chile paste using a large spoon or fork, and cook another 2 minutes or so, or until well incorporated. Add the clams (if you wish to keep them separate, add the diggers first, followed by the necks). Cook about 1 to 2 minutes, or until they reach your desired doneness, stirring from time to time. Add the coconut milk and mix well. Stir in a squeeze or two of lime juice, and add salt and pepper to taste. Remove the pan from the heat, garnish with basil, and serve with rice.

CHAPTER 10

WILL'S FIRST CLAM

Back at the condo, Rich and I laid down our nets. Rich was a longtime friend and fellow razor clam aficionado, and we had finally managed to go clamming together. Our nets were round as pumpkins from the morning's dig. Rich's son, Will, eight, came out and admired our haul. Rich asked if he wanted to go to the beach and dig a clam. Now, Will had been to the beach many times razor clamming with his folks, but mostly he had played while Mom and Dad did the serious work. He had yet to catch his first clam, I was told.

"You haven't dug a clam?" I asked, surprised.

"No," his dad answered. "Maybe today will be the day."

Will didn't say anything, just looked shy and doubtful. Then he said he might go to the beach, maybe even dig a clam, but he didn't want to hold it.

"Are they too icky?" I asked. I wanted to say, hey, razor clams aren't slimy; the shells are smooth and glossy, and the flesh is pleasantly pliant. But I tried to see it like an eight-year-old boy, and yes, you'd have to say they were icky and weird.

Will clambered into his waders, hand-me-downs from his sister with diminutive waterproof feet and suspenders. "Do you want to drive or walk to the beach?" Rich asked. I thought for sure Will would

Will with razor clam

want to go by car, but no, he wanted to walk. So the three of us headed along the trail toward the beach. It was the second time Rich and I walked past the short pine trees that morning, through the sandy dunes and beach grass, and back to the ocean's steady rumble.

The tide was past the low, and the shore looked like a war zone. There were holes and piles of sand everywhere from the digging. A crow was strutting along inspecting, hoping for a meal, while a seagull pecked a broken clam someone had discarded. Another gull watched intently, and soon the two birds were arguing. The tide was coming in but there was still plenty of beach, and the clams were showing with abandon. "Now we're going to look for holes," Rich said to the small figure beside him. "Let me show you what a good hole looks like."

They found a show and Rich positioned his son between the clam and the surf. Will started digging with a short-handled shovel. He put his foot on the blade and took a scoop. It was more like digging a hole to plant a tree than proper use of the clam gun, but it was razor clamming.

"Keep going," said Dad. "He's deep." Now, when you use the shovel in this way, there's a good chance of cracking the shell or

WILL'S FIRST CLAM 163

slicing through the siphon. But Will dug in small sips, and the sand was hard, so you could see the tunnel-like hole left behind by the retreating siphon. Rich reached in the hole, deep, and explored around.

"He's right here," he said to Will.

"I don't want to touch it," Will answered. So Rich grabbed it, a nice five-inch clam, washed it in a nearby puddle, and handed it over. Will reached out with stubby munchkin fingers, took the clam, and held it at arm's length. "Your first clam!" said Rich.

But Will wasn't done. He started digging a second hole. Rich encouraged him in a way that made me think he was the best father ever. "Okay, now scoop. Good. Four more like that and I'll reach in there. Good. One more and I'll put my hand in there."

Rich looked for it in the muddy hole, the same gray flat color as the sky. "Okay, it's right here."

This time Will put his hand into the soup and pulled out a clam. "I've officially got one clam now," he said.

We looked around for another hole to dig, and Will set to work with every part of his being, leaning into the shoveling. He made a good hole and Rich looked for the clam, but he couldn't find it. "He's gone to China now," said Will.

The next show was a classic keyhole, large and round as if a fat pencil had stabbed the sand and withdrawn, and I thought there must be a giant clam in there. Will started digging in his intense way, and he said, while digging, "I think I might grab him." The hole slowly filled with opaque water and the sides caved in some. Rich reached in and said, "I can feel him bubbling."

This time, Will stuck his hands deep into the dark water and sand, and searched around. Then he withdrew his arm and, with a long, slow sucking sound, out came his hand and the clam. Will held the brown-gold streamlined beauty and said, with a whiff of exasperation, "Finally, I got my first clam all by myself."

Soon he started in on another hole. "I want to do it all myself," he said. Rich advised him not to start digging too close to the clam show, or he'd break the shell. Will took a shovelful and there was a thin marine worm. "Look, an earthworm," he said, and kept digging. The clam was not moving, and we could see the tip of the siphon. His dad said, "Use your hands. Scoop like a dog."

"I might not be strong enough to dig like that."

"Scoop, scoop like a dog."

Will complied, tossing sand left and right.

"There it is. He looks huge," said Dad. Will pawed around the hole and came up with the clam.

"That was awesome," Rich said. "Like Iron Man digging. We have four."

"We still have eleven more?" said Will.

Around this time Will's mother, and his teenage sister, appeared. Will held up the four clams to show Mom. "Nicely done," she said.

"How about we get the limit!" he said.

We all moved to the surf. Most people were heading home, except for a few perch fishermen who stood knee-deep in the water, holding their long poles baited with clam necks from the morning dig. There were still plenty of clam signs on the beach, and even some clams necking, their siphon tips opening and closing like banshees, and spurting water. Will continued digging. His little fists were pink from cold, and his arms wet. Dad was still coaching. "Turn around," he said. "Always dig behind the clam."

"Watch out, a wave!" Rich held Will by the scruff of his jacket as the dark water swirled about Rich's calves and Will's thighs. It stayed a long time and then slowly sucked back out, becoming a sheen of rivulets, and all the while Rich held Will's coat like a human construction crane. Rich reached into the now-filled hole up to his shoulder. "I got it," he said, and handed the clam to Will, who dropped it into the net and did a victory dance, skipping along the beach with his hands in the air.

"Five more!" shouted Will. "I'm not at all worn out."

Will and Dad with the haul

I asked Will if he likes to eat clams.

"No," he said, "but now I think I will."

The shore was nearly devoid of people, the bulk had returned back to the comforts of civilization. We were still at the beach, letting the surf curl around our wader-protected feet and ankles. Will staggered around, insisting on getting a limit. The tide was rolling deeply in and out again on the ever-so-flat beach. The low was definitely over. Sea fingers smoothed the gray mounds of sand, filling the foxholes and returning the beach to its pristine planar expanse.

Will was standing in front of another hole. I thought how lucky he was, on this first dig, to have the clams showing so readily and obviously. There was no prospecting, no wrist-wrenching thumping of the beach like some mad John Henry. The little fellow lined up with another hole, holding the shovel that was just about as long as he is, and he said, "Let the digging race begin."

Soon it was time to count the haul. Rich laid the clams on the beach and Will counted, one, two, three . . . . seven, eight . . . . thirteen, fourteen. "We need one more." His hands were red and wet, but he seemed oblivious. The beach was now ours except for the occasional beach stroller. With great determination Will found his last clam. He attacked with abandon, tossing the sand to the left and right. In short order, the glossy brown fifteenth clam was in the net.

"Let's go wash our hands a little," said Will in his small eight-year-old voice. "They're ruined." Will and Dad walked to the water's edge and rinsed, two dark shapes under the overcast sky.

We started back up the beach for the walk home. As we walked we saw more holes, and Will said, "Let's get another. . . . Oh wait, you're not allowed."

"Fifteen is plenty," said Dad, who no doubt was thinking of the clam cleaning that Will was certainly not going to do, at least not today. Wolves know when to stop—they hunt for the week's meal—but we humans immerse in the sheer pleasure of success and the joy of abundance, and the corrals of regulation and allotted numbers barely hold us. With each step the heavy net bounced on Rich's thigh like a tetherball.

Back at the room, Rich dumped the clams into the sink. A few necks squirmed and feet twisted this way and that. "They're still alive?" Will asked.

"They're all alive," said Rich. Will looked at them in puzzlement and curiosity.

Will marched on to his next round of activities. An hour at the beach completed, on a sliver of coastal wildness atop a city of clams. He will likely be clamming for the rest of his life, I thought to myself. I wondered if, fifty years from this day, he might not find himself at this very beach, thinking back to the time when he hung out with his dad and some other guy, put his hand into a muddy hole, saw a worm in the sand, and got a limit just like them. And who knows what other razor clam memories will crowd in, tripping over one another like the ocean waves lapping and overlapping.

MARIE'S "FEED THE CROWD" CHOWDER
Makes 6 to 8 servings

This New England–style recipe comes courtesy of Marie O'Connell, who originally hailed from Boston and is now matriarch of Rich and Will's razor clamming family. Quick and tasty when hungry diggers want food, says Amy, Rich's wife, who is also an accomplished clammer.

- 3 tablespoons vegetable oil
- 3 large yellow onions, diced
- 4 stalks celery, diced
- 8 razor clams, diced (about 2 cups)
- 4 (10.75-ounce) cans condensed cream of potato soup
- 6 cans regular milk (measured using 10.75-ounce soup can)
- Salt and freshly ground black pepper
- Pat of butter (optional)

In a large soup pan, heat the oil and sauté the onions and celery over medium-high heat. When soft and cooked through, about 5 minutes, add the clams. Sauté very briefly until just starting to firm. Add the soup and milk, mix well, and cook until heated through. Add salt to taste and a generous amount of pepper. Add the butter, if desired, for added richness.

KAREN'S RAZOR CLAM DIP
Makes 4 to 6 servings

Karen grew up eating clam dip. On Friday nights, her dad would mix a can of chopped clams with cream cheese and they'd settle in to eat clam dip and watch TV. Friday-night treat night. It was one of the few things she could count on since her family moved every couple of years as her father was transferred around the country. When Karen discovered razor clams, she was thrilled: the flavor was so much better than ordinary canned clams.

- 1 teaspoon olive or vegetable oil
- 1 teaspoon unsalted butter
- 1 cup minced razor clams with their juice (fresh or frozen)
- 1 (8-ounce) package good-quality cream cheese, softened
- 1½ tablespoons chopped fresh chives
- Scant ⅛ teaspoon Worcestershire sauce
- Scant ⅛ teaspoon lemon juice
- Salt and pepper to taste
- 2 tablespoons minced Italian flat-leaf parsley (optional)

Chips or veggie sticks, for serving

Heat the oil and butter in a medium-sized fry pan over medium heat, then add the minced clams and sauté briefly until just cooked and firmed, 20 seconds to 1 minute or so. Remove from the heat and allow to cool. When cool, add the clams and their liquid to the cream cheese. Add the chives, Worcestershire sauce, and lemon juice and mix well. Add salt and pepper to taste. Chill the dip (preferably for 24 hours in the refrigerator, to allow the flavors to blend). Garnish with parsley, if desired, and serve with chips or veggie sticks.

CODA
PRACTICAL MATTERS

GETTING STARTED

It's great if you have someone to show you the razor clamming ropes, but if not, websites and online videos provide loads of useful information. The Washington, Oregon, and Alaska Departments of Fish and Wildlife all have websites with information on how to identify shows and dig razor clams, as do sport lodges and individual devotees.

The Long Beach and Ocean Shores razor clam festivals offer information and sometimes workshops. You can always grab someone on the beach as well. Folks are usually pretty friendly.

Of course, you will also need a shellfish license and a shovel or tube to dig clams. It's reasonable to start with cheaper tools and see if you like the activity. A brightly colored hat or coat helps keep track of friends and family members. Similarly, a flag on the car can be helpful.

It's good practice to keep an eye on the ocean while clamming. Waves can come in unpredictably. It's fun to work in pairs or small groups, helping one another spot clam shows and keep lookout.

Cleaning clams in the clam kitchen. The oblongs of the opened shells look like angel wings.

CLEANING AND KEEPING CLAMS

It's best to clean and eat your catch within forty-eight hours. If you can't, rubber-banding the clams so the valves stay closed and putting them on ice or in the coldest part of the fridge is a good idea. They'll stay alive for five days, and, while they may look sad on the fifth day, they are still edible. Don't keep live clams in freshwater; they will die and the necks will go flaccid.

Unlike hard-shell clams, there's no need to purge razor clams of sand before cooking, because you are going to open and thoroughly clean them.

Cleaned clams freeze reasonably well. Whole clams in the shell freeze well, too; some think this method better preserves the fresh taste of the clam. But whole clams take up more room in the freezer and, of course, have to be cleaned upon defrosting.

Websites and videos are good references for learning how to clean a clam. The basic idea is to cut away all the dark parts. When cutting around the stomach, be careful not to sever the two small bits of

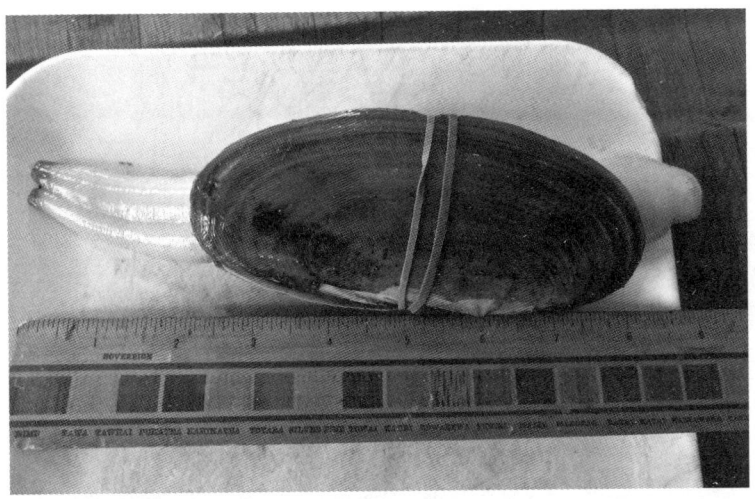

Rubber bands help the razor clam stay closed and keep. As the clam weakens, the adductor muscles can no longer constrain the hinge, which is "spring-loaded" to open the clam shell.

connecting tissue from the foot if you want the clam whole. Halve the foot from its backside for the same purpose.

Information on how to preserve clams in mason jars via pressure canning is available from state university extension agents.

DRIVING ON THE BEACHES

Driving on the beach is fun, but avoid the soft "sugar" sand high up on the beach. It's easy to get stuck there. If you do get stuck, don't gun the tires; you'll bury the axle and make rescue that much harder.

A good strategy is to follow the high tide line, usually marked by seaweed and other detritus. The sand there is generally damp and firm. Often it's convenient to drive in other people's tracks. Four-wheel drive is beneficial. Some people let a little air out of their tires for better traction.

Washington considers the beach a state highway (speed limit twenty-five miles per hour; watch out for sunbathers and beach debris). The highway begins where the county road ends. Oregon also allows driving on its beaches, but to a lesser extent.

At low tide, it's illegal to drive on the lower beach, where the razor clams live, because the car's weight could crush baby clams.

Kalaloch is the only beach that has no car access. You have to walk down steep paths from the high bluffs above. Kalaloch is entirely within the coastal portion of Olympic National Park.

ENFORCEMENT

Fish and Wildlife officers have the same general police powers as other law enforcement officers. If the game warden asks to see your clams, comply or you may face fines for failure to submit for inspection. It's equivalent to a cop pulling you over and asking for your driver's license.

The Supreme Court of Washington reworked court rules in 2012 in response to general concerns about inadequate due process in misdemeanor cases. Few people understood that pleading guilty to a misdemeanor and paying the fine, technically called bail forfeiture, could turn up as a criminal record when applying for a job or housing.

In place of bail forfeiture, the court substituted mandatory court appearances. The court reasoned that this would help people better understand their rights and the consequences of a guilty plea. But for razor clammers, the new process meant even one clam over the limit required an appearance in court.

State fisheries officials recognized that the new regime was perhaps inflexible and disproportionate to the offense, and they persuaded the legislature to allow leeway for officers to write up lesser fishing and hunting violations as an infraction, similar to a speeding ticket. The fine in 2015 was $150, but the transgression wouldn't appear as a criminal record and red flag for potential employers or landlords.

In cases of more egregious violations—say, digging more than two limits—officers don't feel they have discretion. "That's just flat out poaching," says Captain Dan Chadwick. "You talk to the judge." Such major violations constitute gross misdemeanors, with penalties of up to five thousand dollars and/or 364 days in jail.

Penalties can be stiff for even just a few clams over the limit if you have a prior record, but everything depends on the particular court. "I just had a guy, he failed to produce his clams when asked," said Chadwick. "When he finally did, he was eight over the limit. I wrote him a ticket. He was a repeat offender from a number of years ago, and the judge fined him $750."

It's all at the judge's discretion. And the wildlife officer can send you to court for even one clam over.

Basic advice? Don't poach. Dig a limit. If asked to show your catch, do so. In many cases, the officer already knows if you've committed a violation, thanks to spotting scopes, binoculars, night vision goggles, citizen informants, and a pretty good sense of what doesn't look right based on years of observation. Officers can get annoyed when people lie or deny the obvious. "I haven't dug clams yet," someone might say when wet and covered with sand.

Officer Loc Do spent a half hour peering at two women through a spotting scope when I went with him on razor clam patrol one weekend morning. He clamped the scope to his truck's halfway-rolled-down window and watched from the comfort of the driver's seat. Without the scope, the women were just two dots near the surf. With the scope, he was able to keep a log of their actions. Later we drove over and contacted them. They denied burying clams. "I saw you burying one with your left hand at 7:42," said Officer Do, consulting his log. They were a mother and daughter team that had come up from Oregon to dig clams, and they protested their innocence. The mother explained that the daughter had knee issues, and the mom looked none too steady herself. Officer Do ended up explaining to them about disability licenses. No ticket was issued even though, as he pointed out to me later, their clams were all large and intact, an unlikely scenario.

Over the years, razor clam enforcement has veered between emphasizing education and keeping the letter of the law; of late, the stress is more on the latter. Most officers are looking for major offenders. Compliance seems to be increasing overall, or so I'm told.

A more subtle case of rule breaking is using the license of a young family member as an excuse for an extra fifteen clams. The state finally added a video to its razor clam website to clarify the rules about teaching a young person to dig; essentially, a youngster needs to be actively taking part.

There are many ways to cheat, of course, and every wildlife cop has stories. The waders stuffed with 225 clams, so that the sweet old couple looked like two Michelin Men. The poached clams that couldn't be found, until the officer looked under the car and discovered hidden tubes attached to the chassis. The woman with plastic bags safety-pinned to the inside of her coat: as she dug, she added one clam to the net, one to the bag. One ambitious poacher caught his limit, drove to another location, exchanged his red flannel jacket for a green fleece, and set about getting a second limit. "But he forgot to change his dog," the game warden grinned.

And, of course, when clamming with friends or spouse, the temptation for the better digger to put golden eggs into the laggard's net is great. I have fifteen clams banging in the net on my hip, and you have only three! The rule requires everyone to dig his or her own clams, but when one party has an aching back, and the other party would gladly dig all day long . . . well, you can believe the handful of game wardens can't keep all this under control, not with five management areas, fifty-three miles of beach, and thousands of diggers.

No, ultimately the only way these rules and the resource can be sustained is internal compliance. What I call the Mantra. The limit has been the same for more than forty years, and the rules are repeated so often by authorities and the media that they roll off the tongue like a catechism: the limit is fifteen, you must keep the first fifteen dug regardless of size or condition, and each person must dig their own clams. The Mantra.

BEACH NAMES, MOCROCKS, AND OTHER CONFUSIONS

Beach names can be confusing. There are individual beach names, group beach names, beaches identified by the name of the beach access road, and beach management area names. All are used; there are multiple ways to refer to the same destination, and the same name can have various meanings.

The management area names of Long Beach and Twin Harbors are easily understood as terms that derive from major geographic features. The management area names of Kalaloch and Copalis are likewise straightforward, deriving from Native American place names.

The fifth management area, though, is a mash-up that was created by state authorities when they devised the management areas. *Mocrocks* is neither English nor Native, but a Franken-word. Authorities combined the "Moc" of Moclips, the city marking the area's

Clammers enjoying a gentle surf on a very flat beach north of Ocean Shores

northern boundary—and dividing the word oddly since it's pronounced MO-clips—with the "rocks" of Copalis Rocks, the feature marking the southern boundary.

Mocrocks. Most people pronounce this as "Mock-rocks," equal stress on both syllables, so it sounds more like an incantation than a location.

Periodically, somebody wants to rationalize beach or management area names, but this pursuit never goes anywhere.

AIRPORT ON THE BEACH

Do you have a friend who flies a small plane? If so, get him or her to fly you to the airstrip on the hard sand of Copalis Beach, smack dab in the middle of a popular razor clamming destination.

According to accepted wisdom, Don Eastvold was the person responsible for the Copalis State Airport. He had been Washington's attorney general, but after leaving office he found his true calling as a developer of resort sites and became one of the original Ocean Shores investors. He made the airport a reality, or so it's understood.

Copalis appears to be the only airport in the continental United States on a beach, and possibly the only beach airport in the world not on an island. Certainly, it's the only one where you can step out of a plane and dig razor clams.

Pilots love the thrill of landing on a scenic Pacific coast beach about ten miles north of Ocean Shores, where the Copalis River enters the Pacific Ocean. They fret that the airstrip may one day be closed, given that it is within the North Beach Seashore Conservation Area and adjacent to a national marine sanctuary.

The airstrip is marked with a few hard-to-see poles. Pilots should look carefully for people, cars, and driftwood before touching down, and sign the guest book after landing.

EARTHQUAKE AND TSUNAMI RISK

An earthquake and accompanying tsunami could really ruin a nice day of razor clamming. The tourist industry doesn't like to talk about such things. The predictions are pretty awful, but there are measures that can be taken to increase your odds of survival.

Basic strategy: get to higher ground. Consider your evacuation route ahead of time and take note of the ubiquitous tsunami evacuation route signs. Evacuation won't be easy. The beach and other areas will liquefy to quicksand, and your car will start to sink. Roads will buckle and flood. There'll be traffic jams and accidents. Whether in town or on the beach, the car will likely be of little use.

If you feel a major earthquake while at the coast, wait for the shaking to stop, then proceed inland as best as you can to safer elevations. Don't gaggle at the receding sea. Leave your gear. Don't check the news. In the event of a tsunami, it could be five to fifteen minutes between the shaking and walls of water. Find somewhere over thirty feet in elevation, but forty feet is better, because the earth may—will—subside six to eight feet. Climb a tree, get atop a building, walk up a big hill.

Tsunami warning signs are ubiquitous around coastal razor clamming areas.

Prepare to stay a while, at least twenty-four hours, say the experts. You don't know how many waves will come in a tsunami event, but there's always more than one, and the first one is not the biggest.

Don't be fatalistic. There might be a hill nearby, or perhaps a structure or tree. Consider choosing a motel and spending your nights where evacuation is practical.

CLIMATE CHANGE AND OCEAN ACIDIFICATION

Razor clammers worry about climate change, and everybody wants to know what ocean acidification, one of its evil stepchildren, might do to the razor clams. Ocean acidification is caused by rising levels of atmospheric carbon dioxide from our fossil-fueled lives dissolving into seawater, making the water more acidic and thus more difficult for mollusks and other creatures to build their shells.

So far, no one has directly researched the effect of local ocean acidification on razor clams, though the tribulations of other native Northwest shelled creatures, such as pteropods, a kind of snail, have been documented. State biologists hope to conduct studies on razor clams. In recent years, razor clam populations have been healthy, and sometimes outstanding, despite climate change and ocean acidification. But if additional acidity came at just the wrong moment—say, when larval razor clams were forming their shells—or if a more acidified ocean condition became worse or chronic, as seems all too likely, the results could be heart wrenching.

Another concern is hypoxia events, which occur when oxygen-depleted water causes die-offs of organisms including razor clams, fish and crab. Die-offs have been observed on QIN beaches. They appear related to shifts in wind and current patterns due to climate change; these in turn influence the patterns of oxygen-depleted water upwelling from the deep ocean. Environmental changes are difficult to assess, but there's plenty to give a razor clammer pause.

ARE RAZOR CLAMS GOOD FOR YOU?

Clams are a high-protein, low-fat food rich with minerals and vitamins, including iron. Razor clams vary in their mineral content depending on the local environment. "Seafood is what it eats," says Doris Hicks, a thirty-year veteran of seafood nutritional analysis.

Health departments conduct tests for domoic acid and other marine toxins, especially in Washington, which has perhaps the most robust testing program in the nation. The U.S. Food and Drug Administration sets the domoic acid safety threshold at 20 parts per million so that even the weakest members of society will not be harmed. But some researchers suspect that chronic exposure to low levels of domoic acid—or even occasional exposure, when it comes to fetal development—could also be harmful. Pregnant women might exercise caution.

Q&A: STEAMING, TENDERIZING, AND UMAMI

Why not steam the razor clams in the shell, like hard-shell clams?
You could, in theory. But virtually everybody cleans razor clams before cooking, removing not only sand but the gills, stomach, and

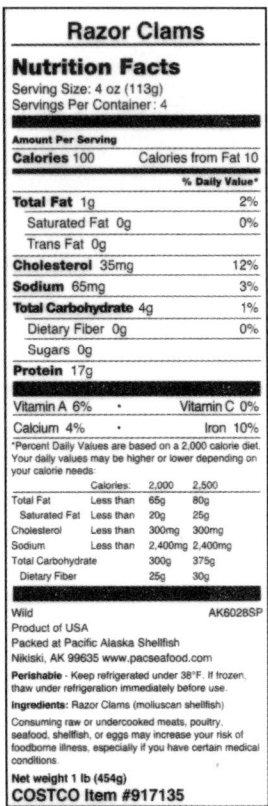

Nutrition label from commercially packed Alaska razor clams

other viscera where marine toxins such as paralytic shellfish poison and domoic acid concentrate, and that's how health authorities test them, grinding up samples of cleaned clams from each management area. Whatever liquid or other benefit might be gained by steaming them whole is probably not worth the potential health risk. However, you could steam the clam meat after it is cleaned. And shucking clams raw is one way to gain a few extra drops of clam liquor.

I think the neck is too tough. Can it be tenderized?

Whack whack whack. I tried tenderizing the neck with a mallet. It made nothing tender and debased the texture.

What gives razor clams their distinctive flavor?

That's hard to say; it's just the way they taste. However, razor clams, like all clams, are high in umami. Defined by the Japanese in 1908, and gaining ground ever since as the fifth basic taste, umami is the savory taste imparted by glutamate, a type of amino acid, and various ribonucleotides. Two characteristics of umami are the mouth-watering sensation and long-lasting tongue-coating feel. Umami is a subtle quality that enhances other flavors. Clams are high in umami substances, notably glutamate, and that can make razor clam dishes seductive to the palate even when the clam flavor is not pronounced.

FUN WITH SHELLS

Alan Rammer, the former state fisheries educator, says that open razor clam shells resemble butterflies. He likes to spray the outside with fixative to preserve them, placing the shells golden-side up on newspaper. The fixative runs a little, which helps keep the periostracum and edges of the shell intact as well as shiny.

Clams have growth rings, but they can be hard to see. Peeling off the periostracum and holding the shell up to the light will often reveal the stages of growth, similar to tree rings. This is less obvious on Washington's clams, which grow year-round, and more pronounced in Alaskan clams, which grow more seasonally.

STATE CLAM

Washington has a state tree, a state amphibian, a state vegetable, and a state endemic mammal. It does not have a state clam. Attention, elementary school students of Pacific and Grays Harbor Counties!

(Western hemlock, Pacific chorus frog, Walla Walla sweet onion, and Olympic marmot, respectively, in case you were wondering.)

APPENDIX 1

WASHINGTON STATE RAZOR CLAM PERSONAL-USE REGULATIONS, 1929–2016

YEAR	BAG LIMIT	LEGAL SIZE	SEASON
To 1929	None	None	None
1929–1942	36 clams/person	3½ inches	None
1943–1947	36 clams/person	None	March 1–September 30
1948–1959	24 clams/person (except 18 in 1950)	None	March 1–September 30
1960–1972	18 clams/person	None	March 1–September 30
Beginning in 1973, beaches closed to razor clamming over the summer.			
1973–1983	15 clams/person	None	October 1–March 15 March 16–June 30, a.m. tides only Multiple special conservation closures Beginning in 1979 razor clam license required
1984–1985			Beaches closed due to NIX infection—no clams

(CONTINUED)

YEAR	BAG LIMIT	LEGAL SIZE	SEASON
1986	15 clams/person	None	February 15–April 4, odd days only October 15–December 15, odd days only

Beginning in 1987, beaches were open in spring and fall, and opened or closed independently according to number of clams.

1987–1995	15 clams/person	None	Spring season: approximately mid-March–mid-May, odd days only, a.m. tides only after 1988 Fall season: approximately mid-October–mid-November, odd days only, p.m. tides only after 1988 Multiple special conservation closures Beginning in 1993 general shellfish license required

Beginning in 1996, beaches were open in fall, winter, and spring, October through May, on specific days each month, favoring minus tides and weekends, and opened or closed independently according to number of clams.

1996–2016	15 clams/person	None	Approximately mid-October–mid-March: a few to many days each month during the best low tide series (typically p.m.) Mid-March–mid-April or May: a few to many days each month during the best low tide series (typically a.m.)

The daily bag limit has remained at fifteen since 1973, more than forty years. Beaches were all or mostly closed in 1992, 1999–2000, and 2002–2003 due to high levels of domoic acid (which can lead to amnesiac shellfish poisoning, or ASP). Table compiled from special reports from the Washington Department of Fish and Wildlife, as well as from newspaper stories and individuals. A more fine-grained accounting of the regulations, especially the seasons, would entail scores of special notes.

APPENDIX 2
RECREATIONAL RAZOR CLAM LICENSE INFORMATION IN WASHINGTON, 1982–1993

Washington instituted a license requirement for razor clamming in 1979. It lasted until 1993, when the license was restructured to include other shellfish, crab, and seaweed. Only for this one brief fifteen-year window is there specific information about the number of individual razor clammers and how many came from out of state, and thus better characterization of the razor clamming phenomenon.

The table on the following page covers twelve years, not the full fifteen, and was a tiny part of a report that concerned the 1993 salmon harvest, as well as that year's sturgeon, bottomfish, and shellfish harvests. Washington Department of Fish and Wildlife was unable to find complete records despite repeated public record requests, only this one table.

As it happens, 1982–1993 was a turbulent and transitional period for razor clams, first because of the bacterium called NIX, which caused clam die-off beginning in late summer 1983, and in later years because of closures from marine biotoxins. The 1982–1983 license year, just before NIX, was the most typical year in the atypical period that

Table 3. SPORT RAZOR CLAM LICENSES SOLD IN WASHINGTON

YEAR	$2.50 RESIDENT LICENSE	$3.00 RESIDENT LICENSE	$10.00 NON-RESIDENT LICENSE	TOTAL LICENSES	TOTAL REVENUE
1982-83	118,933	0	20,872	139,805	$506,053
1983-84	0	0	0	0	0
1984-85	0	0	0	0	0
1985-86	69,767	0	3,105	72,872	$205,468
1986-87	58,885	0	4,708	63,593	$194,293
1987-88	58,877	0	3,590	57,000	$178,193
1988	68,138	0	3,969	72,107	$210,035
1989	67,267	0	4,126	71,393	$209,428
1990	0	68,380	4,388	72,768	$249,020
1991	0	70,108	6,776	76,884	$278,084
1992	0	19,740	293	20,003	$62,150
1993	0	62,810	4,965	67,775	$238,080

Recreational Razor Clam License Information in Washington, 1982-1993. Marianna Alexandersdottir, Patrick Cox, and Wendy Beeghley-White, Washington State Sport Catch Report for Foodfish 1993 (Washington: Department of Fish and Wildlife, 1995)

was about to unfold; in that license year some 119,000 residents, or about 3 percent of the state's 4.3 million population, bought licenses.

Nonresidents bought 21,000 licenses, or about 15 percent of the total. For the overall twelve-year period, nonresidents averaged 8 percent of the licenses bought (it ranged from 3 to 15 percent).

The Washington Department of Fish and Wildlife says on its razor clam web page that the state's beaches have seen "upwards of 300,000 individual diggers" in a year. This is legacy text written years ago by razor clam authorities who presumably had access to the complete razor clam license data 1979 to 1993. I surmise that the 300,000 individual digger figure came from 1979, the year when digger trips reached an all-time high of nearly one million (967,000). Assuming 8 percent of those were nonresidents, that means 276,000 were resident diggers, or 7 percent of the state's population of 4 million. A very significant percentage of the state's residents were kicking up their heels and digging razor clams.

At this time, and until 1986, Fish and Wildlife counted digging trips by the calendar year, whereas licenses were sold seasonally. Comparing licenses sold and number of digging trips—and thus determining the number of digging trips per license—requires reasonable assumptions. In 1982 there were 621,000 digging trips; in 1983 there were 473,000. This gives us an average of 550,000 digger trips for the 1982–1983 season, and 140,000 licenses were sold—roughly four razor clam digging trips per license.

From 1983 to 1985, razor clamming was canceled due to the NIX disease and lack of clams, and hence there were no license sales. In 1992 license sales were low because the beaches were mostly closed to razor clamming due to the biotoxin domoic acid (causing ASP).

Looking for clam shows. Courtesy Donna Sharrett

RECIPES

BASIC SAUTÉED RAZOR CLAMS	21
SAUTÉED RAZOR CLAMS IN BROWN BUTTER	22
SAUTÉED RAZOR CLAMS WITH CAPERS	23
"CLAMILY FRITTERS"	38
CLAMS WITH SNAP PEAS IN CHAMPAGNE VINAIGRETTE	53
SILVEY FAMILY FRIED RAZOR CLAMS	71
KAREN'S FRY MIX	73
A VINTAGE CHOWDER	87
"FRESH CLAM BALLS"	88
"CLAMSHELL RAILROAD" CLAMS CHOWDER	107
DAN'S LOW-FAT CLAM CHOWDER	123
LEE'S RAZOR CLAM CHOWDER	124
BROCK'S RAZOR CLAMS WITH BLACK BEAN SAUCE	143
CHOPPED CLAMS WITH MISO	159
RAZOR CLAM CEVICHE	160
COCONUT MILK CURRY CLAMS WITH BASIL	161
MARIE'S "FEED THE CROWD" CHOWDER	169
KAREN'S RAZOR CLAM DIP	170

NOTES

CHAPTER 1. INTRODUCTIONS

17 **during a recent season:** The season was 2013–2014. There were 451,046 digger trips.

18 **summer digs have been off limits:** Clams in the summer are also less desirable because the clams lose body weight after spawning, and the bulk of spawning in Washington takes place in the spring, from April to May.

21 **tasty, but may be tough:** Ivar's dinner menu, 1966, Pacific Shellfish Ephemera, Matt Winters Digital Collection. Contact Matt Winters at mwinters@chinookobserver.com for information and permission to view the online Flickr album.

CHAPTER 2. LAY OF THE LAND

24 **Ocian in view O! The joy:** The intrepid duo misunderstood their position when Clark wrote his famous statement and were actually still just short of the Pacific Ocean. For more on the quote, see, for example, *The Lewis and Clark Journey Log*, leg 13, www.nationalgeographic.com/lewisandclark/journey_leg_13.html, part of the NationalGeographic.com website. Oddly, the quote from Clark's journal is variously reported. LewisandClarkTrail.com provides the quote verbatim; see the November 7, 1805, entry at http://lewisandclarktrail.com/section4/wacities/chinook/lewisclarkcenter/1805history1.htm.

26 **wrecked ship The Alice:** Tom Nari, "Shipwrecks at the Mouth of the Columbia River," *USA Today*, http://traveltips.usatoday.com/shipwrecks-mouth-columbia-river-107664.html. *The Alice* sank on January 15, 1909, near Ocean Park, Washington. The ship was overloaded with cement that hardened when the ship sank in shallow waters, keeping the ship upright for decades. For more on shipwrecks around the Long Beach Peninsula, see "Shipwrecks: Graveyards

of the Pacific," Washington's Long Beach Peninsula website, posted April 1, 2010, https://funbeach.com/shipwrecks-graveyards-pacific/.

26 **they borrowed a pan:** Robyn Unruh, "History of the World's Largest Frying Pan and Razor Clam Festival," self-published, 2013, and originally available on the Long Beach Razor Clam Festival website. Updated by Keleigh Schwartz in 2016 and posted on the Long Beach Razor Clam Festival website, "History" page, http://longbeachrazorclamfestival.com/long-beach-razor-clam-festival-history/. Giant frying pans turn out to be a popular civic undertaking around the world. The one at Long Beach is far from the world's largest, and probably wasn't even in 1948.

31 **bought a cattle ranch:** Gene Woodwick, *Images of America: Ocean Shores* (Charleston, SC: Arcadia Publishing, 2010), 7–8, 37, 41, 93. The six-mile-long ranch was owned by Ralph Minard.

31 **An eight-foot-tall razor clam sculpture:** The sculpture, by an unidentified artist, was donated by the Tommer Construction Company. See Woodwick, *Images of America*, 37. Woodwick reports the material as cedar in *Images of America* on p. 2, but Rachel Thomson calls it spruce in "Clam Caper: Who Took the City's Giant Bivalve," July 2009 monthly supplement, *The Daily World* (Aberdeen).

32 **local people worshipped razor clams:** Described in Thomson, "Clam Caper."

34 **hop to the ocean via the beach access roads:** Kalaloch is the only beach that has no car access. You have to walk down steep paths from the high bluffs above. Kalaloch is entirely within the coastal portion of Olympic National Park.

CHAPTER 3. SACRED TREATIES

41 **Fifty-three miles in total:** Clayton Parson, Washington Department of Fish and Wildlife (WDFW) razor clam technician, personal email communication, October 17, 2014. According to Parson, the lengths of the five razor clam management areas, from south to north, are: Long Beach, 24.27 miles; Twin Harbors, 6.17 miles; Copalis, 11.46 miles; Mocrocks, 7.41 miles; and Kalaloch, 4.63 miles.

44 **our all-mighty sacred treaty:** Junior Goodell, "Grays Harbor Oil Terminal Would Threaten Quinault Indian Identity," op. ed., *The Seattle Times*, June 2, 2015.

44 **whose ancestors traditionally razor clammed:** The vicinity of Ocean Shores was used by as many as thirty-two Native American bands. See Gene Woodwick, *Images of America: Ocean Shores* (Charleston, SC: Arcadia Publishing, 2010), 7. The location was a time-honored meeting place for trade and razor clam harvest. See, for example, Norah Berg, *Lady on the Beach*, with Charles Samuels (London: Alvin Redman, 1957), 81.

44 **guaranteed to appear at festivals:** Ed Johnstone, Quinault Indian Nation policy spokesperson, interview with author, September 11, 2014.

44 **large canoes from seventy-five tribes:** Jen Graves, "This Is Not a Tourist Event," *The Stranger*, August 14, 2013.

44 **served razor clams as part of the celebration:** *Northwest Indian Fisheries Commission News*, summer 2013.

45 **treaties of 1854 and 1855 concluded by Isaac Stevens:** See, for example, Alex Tizon, "25 Years After the Boldt Decision—The Fish Tale That Changed History," *The Seattle Times*, February 2, 1999, A-1. The other coastal treaty tribes besides the QIN were the Quileute, Hoh, and Makah.

46 **refused to consider the appeal in 1975:** Ibid. The essence of the Boldt decision was later further affirmed in 1979, when the U.S. Supreme Court refused to hear a collateral case called *Washington v. Fishing Vessel Association*.

46 **extending treaty fishing rights:** Jason W. Anderson, "The World Is Their Oyster? Interpreting the Scope of Native American Off-Reservation Shellfish Rights in Washington State," *Seattle University Law Review* 23, no. 145 (1999): 145–173. Also John Hollowed, Northwest Indian Fisheries Commission (NWIFC), interview with author, September 25, 2015; and Phil Katzen, attorney, interview with author, October 6, 2015. Katzen, one of the many attorneys working on the Rafeedie case on behalf of the tribes, served as co-lead and co-coordinator of the legal team.

47 **Rafeedie's decision was appealed:** "Rafeedie Decision," Northwest Indian Fisheries Commission, http://nwifc.org/about-us/shellfish/rafeedie-decision.

47 **addressed the tidelands of Puget Sound:** Private property owners along the heavily populated Puget Sound shoreline raised an uproar over the Rafeedie decision. The ruling made the shellfish on their tidelands available to tribes, along with the need for property owners to allow access to harvest. Eventually, and painfully, compromises were developed to satisfy all parties regarding implementation.

However, disputes continue being litigated to the present day concerning implementation of the Boldt and Rafeedie decisions, making it "one of the biggest, most complex, and longest running [cases] in the history of the federal judiciary," according to attorney Phil Katzen.

More than forty-five years after the original filing of the Boldt case in May 1970, Katzen, who presented the opening and closing arguments, personally continues to litigate implementation of tribes' treaty fishing and shellfishing rights.

47 **It was a difficult meeting:** Dan Ayres, then shellfish biologist and currently razor clam manager, interview with author, September 9, 2014. Ayres clearly remembers the day the QIN biologist, Curt Holt, walked into the office. Holt now works for the WDFW in the salmon program, but refused to comment on the razor clam history.

47 **those traditional grounds amounted to twenty-three miles:** The traditional razor clamming grounds were actually even greater in extent. According to Pearl Capoeman Baller, past QIN president, the QIN discussed pursuing the right to razor clam all the way to the Columbia River, and thus perhaps virtually all fifty-three miles of Washington's razor clam habitat. But razor clamming is hard work, and ultimately the QIN decided to focus attention on building its off-

reservation tribal casino on trust land near Ocean Shores. Pearl Capoeman Baller, personal email communication, December 17, 2014.

In her memoir *Lady on the Beach,* Norah Berg mentions that the Indians dug razor clams south of Grays Harbor—that is, in the six-mile-long Twin Harbors management area between Grays Harbor and Willapa Bay. See Berg and Samuels, *Lady on the Beach,* 81.

47 **These treaties mean something:** John Hollowed, legal and policy advisor, Northwest Indian Fisheries Commission, interview with author, September 25, 2015.

CHAPTER 4. ECOLOGY AND ANATOMY

55 **Specifically, he found diatoms:** Harvey C. McMillin, "The Life-History and Growth of the Razor Clam," State of Washington Department of Fisheries, 1924.

56 **the trio spent more than a decade:** J. Lewin, C. Schaefer, and D. Winter, "Surf-Zone Ecology and Dynamics," in *Coastal Oceanography of Washington and Oregon,* ed. Michael Landry and Barbara Hickey, 567–594 (Amsterdam: Elsevier, 1989).

Joyce Lewin and Charles Schaefer were from the University of Washington. Donald Winter was from the University of Redlands, California, though he later joined the University of Washington. The three researched surf-zone diatoms continuously from 1971 through 1982. Their study remains one of the most comprehensive and definitive.

57 **rising up and merging with bubbles:** The vertical movement may have something to do with the fine inorganic particles that surf diatoms adorn themselves with, attaching clay minerals like montmorillonite—washed into the ocean by the Columbia River—onto mucilaginous cell coatings, and then shedding them. Various studies cite this behavior as an important adaptation of surf diatoms to the turbulent, shallow water column. See Maria Célia Villac, et al., "Marine Planktonic Diatoms, Including Potentially Toxic Species," in *The Diatom World,* ed. Joseph Seckbach and Patrick Kociolek, 477–478 (Dordrecht: Springer, 2011).

However, other studies say that this is not how these particular diatoms, *Attheya armatus,* control movement in the water column. See, for example, Clarisse Odebrecht et al., "Surf Zone Diatoms: A Review of the Drivers, Patterns and Role in Sandy Beaches Food Chains," *Estuarine, Coastal and Shelf Science,* vol. 150, part A (October 5, 2014), 30. For an abstract, see www.sciencedirect.com/science/article/pii/S0272771413003338.

58 **Those beaches were not quite so long:** Since the research of Lewin, Schaefer, and Winter, some fifty locations around the world have been reported with large surf diatom communities, most in the Southern Hemisphere. See Odebrecht, "Surf Zone Diatoms," 24–35.

58 **the surf diatom that predominates:** The cell walls of *Attheya armatus,* like those of all diatoms, are made of silica, or silicon dioxide, the same material

found in sand or glass. Diatoms thus famously live in glass houses. Diatom shells are symmetrical and often ornate and beautiful. There are at least 30,000 species, and probably as many as 100,000, or even 200,000; it's a matter of debate turning on what constitutes a species. Only a dozen or fewer species of this multitude are surf diatoms.

60 **born either male or female:** There's no way to tell externally if a razor clam is male or female. Gender is determined by examining the reproductive material in the foot. Males have smooth, creamy spawn, while the female spawn is more granular, like small-curd cottage cheese. In practice, it is sometimes hard for an ordinary person to distinguish.

60 **foamy white slick:** Zachary Forster, scientific technician, WDFW, Coastal Shellfish Olympic Region Harmful Algal Bloom (ORHAB) Monitoring Partnership, personal email communication, June 2, 2016. Forster was fortunate enough to see and take pictures of a large spawning event one calm day on Long Beach.

63 **like a myriad of tiny oars:** F. W. Weymouth, H. C. McMillin, and H. B. Holmes, "Growth and Age at Maturity of the Pacific Razor Clam, Siliqua Patula (Dixon)," *Bulletin of the Bureau of Fisheries*, vol. XLI, document no. 984 (Washington, D.C. Government Printing Office, 1925), 206.

64 **a fully rotating part:** Elizabeth Gosling, *Bivalve Molluscs: Biology, Ecology and Culture* (Oxford, UK: Fishing News Books, 2003), 31.

64 **or, as some have called it, "snouting":** See, for example, Norah Berg, *Lady on the Beach*, with Charles Samuels (London: Alvin Redman, 1957), 150.

64 **A letter sent by a man:** William J. Betts, April 23, 1994. The letter was sent to WDFW educator Alan Rammer in response to his public call for razor clam stories and history. The information and interviews gathered by Rammer are now in the razor clam files of the Aberdeen Museum of History.

66 **flares the bottom of its foot:** Rose H. Pohlo, "Morphology and Mode of Burrowing in Siliqua Patula and Solen Rosaceui (Mollusca: Bivalvia)," *Veliger*, vol. 6 (1963): 98–104. Also see the entry for "burrowing" under "Clam Habitats & Ecology" on the website "A Snail's Odyssey," www.asnailsodyssey.com/LEARNABOUT/CLAM/clamHabi.php.

66 **called it the "RoboClam":** Amina Khan, "RoboClam: Robot Inspired by the Razor Clam's Amazing Digging Powers," *Los Angeles Times*, March 5, 2014.

66 **can dig about one centimeter a second:** A. G. Winter, R. L. H. Deits, et al., "Razor Clam to Roboclam: Burrowing Drag Reduction Mechanism and Their Robotic Adaptation," *Bioinspiration and Biomimetics*, April 8, 2014. Also see James Morgan, "'RoboClam' Could Anchor Submarines," *BBC News*, April 10, 2014, www.bbc.com/news/science-environment-26939126.

67 **Timing was everything:** Helen Knight, "Robot Builds on Insights into Atlantic Razor Clam Dynamics," *MIT News*, March 25, 2014, http://news.mit.edu/2014/robot-builds-on-insights-into-atlantic-razor-clam-dynamics. The technique and

timing make the animals' burrowing very efficient, using the equivalent energy of only one AA battery to dig up to half a kilometer.

CHAPTER 5. PAST ABUNDANCES

74   **piled high with mounds:** As, for example, near Ocean Shores. Norah Berg, *Lady on the Beach*, with Charles Samuels (London: Alvin Redman, 1957), 81.

74   **Dixon wrote, "[For a repast]:** George Dixon, *A Voyage Round the World; but More Particularly to the North-West Coast of America*, (London: Geo. Golding, 1789), 354–355. The book consisted mostly of the letters written by Dixon's cargo officer, William Beresford. However, Dixon wrote the introduction and appendixes, source of the quote.

74   **Dixon was the first:** Weymouth, McMillin, and Holmes, "Growth and Age at Maturity," 202.

75   **began his career digging and pickling:** Clarence Sigurdson, "The History of [the] West Coast Razor Clam Industry," unpublished typewritten pages, undated but written circa 1985, at Museum of the North Beach, p. 1.

75   **he developed a special process:** Richard Nickerson, *A Critical Analysis of Some Razor Clam (Siliqua Patula, Dixon) Populations in Alaska*, Alaska Department of Fish and Game, July 1975, p. 1.

Nickerson provides a history of commercial razor clam harvests in Alaska that is useful for understanding the overall development of West Coast commercial clamming and canning. He derived his information primarily from Pacific Fish Yearbooks. Also see "History of the Razor Clam Industry" in the Museum of the North Beach 2015 historical calendar.

75   **he built a mini clam-canning empire:** Halferty's packing operation on the Aberdeen waterfront was hard to miss, what with a steam siren "that could be heard shrieking throughout the Chehalis Valley," according to Margaret Malakoff, *Senior Sunset Times*, November 2012, p. 13 (in the collection of Museum of the North Beach). Malakoff was the granddaughter of one of the managers at Pioneer Canneries.

75   **Pioneer Brand recipe booklet of 1911:** This booklet is in the collection of the Museum of the North Beach, and also Pacific Shellfish Ephemera, Matt Winters Digital Collection. For more on Halferty, see, for example, Roy Vataja, "Nothing New—Keep Clam and Dig On," *The Daily World* (Aberdeen), May 3, 2014.

76   **make its way past the breakers:** P. F. Halferty, "Scenes at Clam Bees in Washington, and P. F. Halferty," *The Seattle Daily Times*, May 16, 1919.

76   **the razor clam somersaulted:** Ibid.

76   **Soon, most every hamlet:** See, for example, "New Clam Cannery at Nahcotta Opens," *The Seattle Times*, April 20, 1914. Also see "Clamming: A Heritage Industry," brochure at the Coastal Interpretive Center, Oceans Shores, WA.

77 **three million pounds of canned razor clams:** Timothy D. Schink, Katherine A. McGraw, and Kenneth K. Chew, *Pacific Coast Clam Fisheries* (Seattle: Washington Sea Grant Program, College of Ocean and Fishery Sciences, University of Washington, 1983), 10, 53.

77 **Diggers were preoccupied with the price:** The Aberdeen Museum of History has handwritten notes from oral history interviews recalling the era. Other details may fade, but clam diggers invariably remember the price paid per pound. Or at least think they do.

77 **Razor clamming was the principal local industry:** Berg and Samuels, *Lady on the Beach*, 80.

77 **The clams were a subsistence food:** Margaret Malakoff, *Senior Sunset Times*, November 2012, p. 13, in the collection of Museum of the North Beach.

77 **seasonal workers called bluebills:** See Woodwick, *Images of America*, 7. In an interview with the author on April 17, 2015, Woodwick distinguished between bluebills—that is, locally based migrant workers—and more general itinerant workers (e.g., fruit tramps).

Writer Robert Jowett attributes the term *bluebills* not to the migratory ducks, but to the hats fruit pickers wore to shade their faces from the sun, but that seems less likely. See Robert Jowett, "'Hoovervilles' by the Sea," *Moclips Ocean Wave* (newsletter), Moclips-by-the-Sea Historical Society, November 2014, vol. 10, no. 4, p. 2.

Woodwick and Jowett, coastal residents, both rely on their own local experience and the conventional wisdom.

78 **mostly from April to July:** "History of the Razor Clam Industry," Museum of the North Beach 2015 historical calendar.

78 **Classes were scheduled around clamming:** Untitled and unattributed newspaper clipping about North Beach public schools from the 1890s through the 1920s, collection of the Museum of the North Beach, written most likely in the late 1960s or early 1970s. Parents built tables, chairs, and a blackboard for the Oyehut school, according to the story. A Civil War veteran and sea otter hunter rigged up a flagpole and supplied a flag. Though many of the people in these beachside enclaves lived on nearly nothing, there was a sense of community. Norah Berg captures that in *Lady on the Beach*, one reason her book has become a local classic.

78 **a story from 1974:** "The Minard Ranch . . . Oyehut, A Landmark, The Way It Used To Be," *Harbor Trader* vol. 1, no. 1 (Aberdeen, October 3–10, 1974), in Coastal Heritage Services, Gene Woodwick Collection. This collection is the personal and quite substantial archive of Ocean Shores–based historian/author Gene Woodwick. The writer of the story, unspecified, interviewed Emma Minard Tanner in her home not far from where the one-room shanty school had stood. At one point, and lasting for three months, Tanner found herself the only student; at other times, the school was so crowded that extra chairs had to be jammed into

the fourteen-foot-square space. The *Harbor Trader* was a short-lived publication, lasting perhaps less than a year, according to Woodwick.

78 **Ragamuffin's Riviera:** The names were noted by Jowett, "'Hoovervilles' by the Sea."

79 **Helene Jake was notorious:** Francis Rosander, QIN elder, interview with author, October 22, 2014. According to Don Hannula's *Seattle Times* story from 1970 about notable diggers, her name also may have been Helen Black. Or perhaps one or the other appellation was a nickname or a married or maiden name. Hannula, with coastal roots, was a capable reporter who later joined *The Seattle Times*'s editorial team, and he wrote and editorialized on razor clams. Don Hannula, "Aberdeen Man Dug 1,091 Pounds on One Tide," *The Seattle Times*, June 21, 1970.

79 **Daisy Ackley kept a diary:** Daisy Ackley, two photocopied pages, undated, from her presumably unpublished diary/memoir "Wagon Wheels A-Rollin," Coastal Heritage Services, Gene Woodwick Collection. Daisy Ackley was working at a cannery in Cordova, Alaska.

80 **Clarence Sigurdson, a cannery manager:** Clarence Sigurdson, "The History of [the] West Coast Razor Clam Industry," unpublished typewritten pages, undated but written around 1985, collection of the Museum of the North Beach, p. 14.

80 **with tracks right on the sand:** The train tracks can be seen in the 1974 John Wayne crime drama movie *McQ*. The beach scenes were filmed on the Pacific coast near Moclips; the car chase scene was filmed at Analyde Gap beach access road. At the time, the tracks had been long unused but still ran along the beach at the base of the cliff and over a trestle. Wayne, as police detective McQ, drives at high speed down the beach access road and into the gap. The plot concerned police corruption and McQ trying to clear his murdered partner's reputation.

81 **a letter from the Razor Clam Canners Association:** The letter is in the collection of the Museum of the North Beach.

82 **That legal effort failed in court:** Schink, McGraw, and Chew, *Pacific Coast Clam Fisheries*, 11.

82 **It resembled an old-fashioned thresher:** Wendell Keene, "Clam Digging Machine Built in 1910," *The Aberdeen Daily World*, January 24, 1964. Other people may have tried to build mechanical harvesters as well; three photographs in the Museum of the North Beach depict a four-wheeled digger on the beach. Little is known about these photos, and who knows, maybe they were an early version from Gage and Croston.

82 **at times unionized:** The Northwest has a long and sometimes radical labor history, including the Seattle General Strike of 1919, the first citywide labor action in America, which was perceived around the world as perhaps signaling a revolutionary moment. A commercial clam diggers' union was created in 1930, according to "History of the Razor Clam Industry" in the Museum of the North Beach 2015 historical calendar.

83   **mechanical equipment was never able to achieve:** Richard Nickerson, *A Critical Analysis of Some Razor Clam (Siliqua Patula, Dixon) Populations in Alaska* (Juneau: State of Alaska, Department of Fish and Game, 1975), 6–7, 199.

83–84   **An astounding estimated 30 to 40 percent:** Schink, McGraw, and Chew, *Pacific Coast Clam Fisheries*, 11.

84   **Mocrocks, was closed in 1968:** Ibid. Also see Herb Tegelberg, Mike Leboki, and Doug Magoon, *The 1968 Razor Clam Fisheries and Sampling Programs* (Olympia: State of Washington, Department of Fisheries, 1969), 2; and Dennis R. Lassuy and Doug Simons, *Species Profiles: Life Histories and Environmental Requirements of Coastal Fishes and Invertebrates (Pacific Northwest): Pacific Razor Clam.* (Washington, D.C.: National Wetlands Research Center, 1989), 8–9.

85   **all he had to look forward to:** Dann Sears, interview with author, August 14, 2014.

85–86   **in 1973, to fifteen, where it remains today:** The fifteen-clam limit is something of a special number; less than that and the whole expedition might hardly seem worthwhile. The bag limit has been fifteen for more than forty years, recognition of its adequacy.

86   **more than 300,000 individuals:** See appendix 2 for a more detailed discussion.

86   **An astounding multitude:** Brad O'Connor, "Clam Beaches Closed," *The Seattle Times*, June 8, 1972. According to this story, "Public interest in razor clams is enormous. On the weekend of May 13 and 14, the department estimated 110,000 diggers on coastal beaches, an all-time record."

The *Seattle Times* story reported 110,000 *diggers* for the weekend, but I'm guessing the reporter meant 110,000 *digger trips*, which is how the department counts and records. So that weekend there were at least 55,000 individual diggers per day. Conflating or confusing diggers and digger trips is easy to do; and of course, for any one day, the count of diggers and digger trips is the same. But for a weekend, it's often one digger making two digger trips.

WDFW does not archive its daily counts, only the seasonal tallies, but it sometimes provided daily or weekend counts to the media (and still does). The minimum of 55,000 diggers that weekend in 1972, let alone the reported 110,000, is an astounding number. For that entire year, WDFW reported 363,000 digger trips. If the story were accurate, that would mean at least nearly a third of the year's total digger trips took place that one weekend—or, really, substantially more, since many of those individual diggers most likely dug both days of the weekend.

Another busy weekend was also reported by Brad O'Connor in "Thousands of Diggers Storm Ocean Beaches," *The Seattle Times*, April 19, 1976. The key sentence in O'Connor's story says: "The agency estimated that more than 60,000 persons dug clams on the coastal beaches Saturday." (April 19 was the Monday following Easter Sunday; *The Times* was an afternoon paper in 1976.)

This story reports 60,000 *persons* as the day's count. Very possibly this is accurate, which would make this the busiest single day of digging I could find on record, assuming I am correct that the May 13–14, 1972, weekend was misreported per above. But it's possible there are errors in this 1976 report as well, and that this was the count of *weekend* digger trips, especially since the weather was poor that weekend—"wind, cold and a rough surf." To put this report in context, in 1976 there were 807,000 digger trips total. If there were, as a guesstimate, 40,000 digger trips on the Saturday and 20,000 on the Sunday, that would be 60,000 digger trips for the *weekend*, or 4.5 percent of the year's total digger trips, which seems plausible. Still, 60,000 on this *single* Saturday, or 7.5 percent of the year's total digging trips, is conceivable. These were the go-go years for razor clamming, and it was Easter weekend, traditionally huge for razor clamming. So, maybe 60,000 individuals did hit the beach that Saturday. And, as noted in chapter 7, calculations based on number of digger trips have to be taken with a dose of salt; it's possible digger trips were undercounted, although the data from the 1970s is considered reliable by WDFW.

86   **praised the chef at Nikko Restaurant:** Alf Collins, "Fresh Today," *The Seattle Times*, June 29, 1983. Collins was a man about town and food writer. Shiro Kashiba, the sushi-bar wizard at Seattle's Nikko Restaurant, was later to open the eponymous Shiro's. Collins also approvingly mentioned Seattle's Mutual Fish, a fish purveyor, as having razor clams in its live tanks.

86   **Seattle restaurants such Ivar's:** Ivar's ad, *The Seattle Times*, June 17, 1977. Ivar's advertised clam strips and clam chowder, along with razor clams. Charlie's ad, *The Seattle Times*, September 27, 1976. Fried razor clams were one of Charlie's full-course dinner entrées according to the ad, which included a menu.

86   **No Northwest regional cuisine:** Alf Collins, "Food Columnist Decries Trends," *The Seattle Times*, October 26, 1983.

CHAPTER 6. THE ERA OF NIX AND DOMOIC ACID

89   **razor clam production plummeted:** Production dropped from 55,000 to 20,000 cases, each case holding 48 one-pound cans. Timothy D. Schink, Katherine A. McGraw, and Kenneth K. Chew, *Pacific Coast Clam Fisheries* (Seattle: Washington Sea Grant Program, College of Ocean and Fishery Sciences, University of Washington, 1983), 52.

90   **The three-months law:** "Clam Industry, Saved by Closed Season, Making Great Strides," *The Seattle Times*, December 5, 1920.

90   **allowed to keep shrank:** Schink, McGraw, and Chew, *Pacific Coast Clam Fisheries*, 11.

91   **decreed frequent emergency closures:** Brad O'Connor, "Clam Beaches Closed," *The Seattle Times*, June 8, 1972.

91   **Clam diggers have a different mentality:** Quoted by Don Hannula, "Clam-Poacher Clampdown—Dealing with a 'Different Breed,'" *The Seattle Times*, October 25, 1985.

92 **understandable cries of anguish:** "Those Berated Clam Fees Are Showing Dividends," editorial, *The Seattle Times*, June 10, 1981.

93 **replenishing a dwindling clam population:** Ibid.

93 **razor-clam-starved Washingtonians:** Don Duncan, "Clams Caused Jams, Lengthy Closure Fueled Craving," *The Seattle Times*, February 7, 1982.

93 **up to their eyeballs in razor clams:** Doug Barker, "Clams Have Had a Riches to Rags History—So Far," *The Daily World* (Aberdeen), September 10, 1989.

94 **picked up a total of six clams:** Doug Underwood, "Clam Mystery Leaves State Digging," *The Seattle Times*, December 10, 1983.

94 **no dead clam bodies or scattered clam shells:** Bill Gordon and Richard W. Larsen, "No Clams, Coast Reacts with Anger, Quiet Agony," *The Seattle Times*, December 10, 1983.

94 **the state canceled the razor clam season:** Doug Underwood, "State Razor Clam Season Is Canceled," *The Seattle Times*, December 9, 1983.

94 **I'll miss it as much as I'd miss my wife:** Peter Rinearson, "Do You Want to See Me Cry?" *The Seattle Times*, December 11, 1983.

94 **It's going to be a disaster down here:** Bill Gordon and Richard W. Larsen, "No Clams, Coast Reacts with Anger, Quiet Agony," *The Seattle Times*, December 10, 1983.

95 **He called it Nuclear Inclusion Unknown:** Ralph Elston, PhD, principal at AquaTechnics Inc., interview with author, October 20, 2014.

96 **they stumbled on a concentration of baby clams:** Don Hannula, "Resurrection of the Razor Clam—Bright New Hope and Lots of Ifs," *The Seattle Times*, September 13, 1985.

96 **vacuumed up billions and billions:** Alan Rammer, one of the biologists helping with the effort, interview with author, August 17, 2014.

96 **It was like the answer to a prayer:** Hannula, "Resurrection of the Razor Clam."

96 **there was nothing happening:** Rammer, interview.

98 **more difference between two clams on a beach:** Dan Ayres, razor clam manager, WDFW, interview with author, July 11, 2014.

99 **We are now managing around NIX:** Eric Stevick, "NIX: We May Never Get to the Bottom of It," *The Daily World* (Aberdeen), September 10, 1989.

99 **we are not seeing long-term recovery:** Barker, "Riches to Rags."

99 **the state's razor clam educator in 1988:** Alan Rammer was well recognized and popular for his lively educational programs. In the mid-1990s he expanded from razor clams to offer general marine resource programs statewide. In 2009 Rammer was let go from WDFW during budget contractions and began working independently. He won the Marine Education Award in 2012 from the National Marine Educators Association.

101 **Then it did some barrel rolls and expired:** William Dietrich, "Case of the Toxic Clams—Mouse Helped Solve Marine Mystery," *The Seattle Times*, March 12, 1992

101 **The health crisis was traced to eating blue mussels:** "Harmful Algal Blooms

Along the North American West Coast Region: History, Trends, Causes and Impacts," *Harmful Algae* 19 (2012): 133–159.

102 **eleven people had mild symptoms:** Frank Cox, Washington Department of Health marine toxin testing coordinator (retired), interview with author, August 24, 2014.

102 **razor clams are slow to depurate:** Razor clams have a protein that binds domoic acid. V. L. Trainer and B. D. Bill, "Characterization of a Domoic Acid Binding Site from Pacific Razor Clam," *Aquatic Toxicology* 69 (2004): 125–132.

102 **didn't open again until November 1992:** In October 1992, there was a paralytic shellfish poisoning (PSP) closing; otherwise, the fishery would have opened in October.

103 **spiked in razor clams from 11.5 to 68 parts per million:** Seattle Times staff, "Toxin Level Means No Clamming on Oregon's Coast," *The Seattle Times*, May 2, 2005.

103 **the safety threshold of 20 parts per million:** 20 parts per million has been the standard for many decades, established by the U.S. Food and Drug Administration. It is considered a conservative standard, set so the weakest members of society will not be harmed. Presumably, healthy adult individuals could handle higher levels. But some researchers suspect that chronic exposure to low levels could also be harmful, and that even occasional exposure could be deleterious to fetal development. See, for example, Kenneth R. Weiss, "Digging for Data," *Los Angeles Times*, July 31, 2006.

103 **Eventually, three scientists:** V. L. Trainer, B. M. Hickey, and R. A. Horner, "Biological and Physical Dynamics of Domoic Acid Production off the Washington U.S.A. Coast," 2002, *Limnology and Oceanography* 47 (2002): 1438–1446.

103 **if a particular Rube Goldberg–like sequence:** Hannah Hickey, "Predicting when Toxic Algae Will Reach Washington and Oregon Coasts," *UW Today*, September 4, 2014, www.washington.edu/news/2014/09/04/predicting-when-toxic-algae-will-reach-washington-and-oregon-coasts/. The article includes helpful graphics and animation.

103 **The blooms of *Pseudo-nitzschia* originate from the south:** Barbara M. Hickey et al, "A Springtime Source Of Toxic Pseudo-Nitzschia Cells on Razor Clam Beaches in the Pacific Northwest," *Harmful Algae* 25 (May 2013): 1–14. For an abstract, see www.sciencedirect.com/science/article/pii/S1568988313000206.

103 **50 miles wide and 150 miles long:** Sandra Hines, "Columbia River Trumps Pacific Ocean When Conditions Are Right," *UW Today*, August 17, 2001, www.washington.edu/news/2001/08/17/.

104 **the amount spent in the 2007–2008 season:** K. Dyson and D. D. Huppert, "Regional Economic Impacts of Razor Clam Beach Closures Due to Harmful Algal Blooms (HABS) on the Pacific Coast of Washington," *Harmful Algae* 9, no. 3 (March 2010): 264–271.

The researchers were with the University of Washington's School of Marine and Environmental Affairs. The $90 per-digger, per-day amount was high compared to some other investigations, but this study is the most in-depth effort to date and the only one to use questionnaires—that is, to go directly to the diggers. The researchers handed out questionnaires to razor clammers over a spring weekend in 2008. As it happened, it was snowing and also occasionally lightning. I had to laugh, picturing the researchers handing out surveys to clammers with hands so cold they could probably barely clutch them. However, of the roughly 450 surveys handed out, one per group of diggers, about half were completed and returned, a very high percentage. One interesting result: per-person expenditures at Long Beach were about twice as high as those at Mocrocks. Presumably this reflects Long Beach as a well-advertised and more-developed tourist destination with fancier amenities.

The responding parties had traveled an average of 110 miles to reach their preferred clamming beach, whether at Mocrocks, Copalis, Twin Harbors, or Long Beach. As the paper noted, overall there was little data describing recreational razor clam revenue or the effect of HAB closures, and this research was a snapshot. The authors suggested further research over multiple openings and years.

104   **the health department canceled nearly 25 percent:** Dan Ayres, "Washington Razor Clam Management, Setting the 2014–2015 Season," 2014, p. 15. Each year's "Setting the Season" report is posted on the WDFW website, http://wdfw.wa.gov/fishing/shellfish/razorclams/seasons_set.html, supplanting the previous year's report.

104   **adjusted to the post-NIX regime:** Why razor clam populations refused to recover after 1985 is anybody's guess. Perhaps NIX had some kind of long-lasting effect—or perhaps ocean conditions were the reason, suggests Ayres—but nobody knows.

104   **a few continuous days during the best low tide series:** For a brief period, digging was allowed on both the a.m. and p.m. low tides, but the daily limit was still fifteen clams. This regulation was misunderstood and abused, and officials quickly realized that the only effective way to enforce the fifteen-clam limit and prevent "double-dipping" was to allow digging on only one tide per day. That rule was not a totally new thing; digging had at times been restricted to one tide per day in earlier regulations, in 1988 or possibly a little earlier.

Understanding the historic rules and restrictions is complicated, in part because it varied from beach to beach and sometimes changed within a season. See, for example, Don Hannula, "Clam-Poacher Clampdown—Dealing with a 'Different Breed,'" *The Seattle Times*, December 25, 1985.

CHAPTER 7. PUMPING AND COUNTING

109   **a newfangled way for counting:** Dan Ayres, WDFW razor clam manager, interview with author, July 11, 2014. The counting effort in Alaska was a collaboration

between bio-mathematician Terry Quinn, Professor David Nelson, and, perhaps most critically, a graduate student, Nicole Szarzi, who later managed razor clams for the Alaska Department of Fish and Game.

Ayres first heard of the pumped-area method when Professor Quinn presented it at a conference on Prince Edward Island in Canada. Ayres was thrilled, and the two talked long into the night in a jazz bar. Later, Ayres visited Alaska to observe the system firsthand.

111 **We were crying the blues:** Ayres, interview.

114 **They establish a starting line:** An accurate population assessment depends on randomness. The pumped-area method incorporates randomness at several junctures, including selection of the transect locations and whether to go north or south for the six holes at each elevation along the transect. A computer program generates the random choices.

116 **Ayres is proud:** Developing the pumped-area method was a team effort, including Doug Simons, then head of the razor clam program, Clayton Parson, and others.

116 **Ayres engaged diggers:** Ayres, interview. According to Ayres, "We used commercial diggers at Long Beach and Twin Harbors, and tribal diggers at Copalis—and they were allowed to sell their clams."

117 **a staff biometrician named Henry Cheng:** Ayres, interview. Cheng was highly talented, says Ayres, and, "it was a huge loss when Henry Cheng left us. He's well known around the world as a shellfish statistician." Cheng ultimately left biological work to join employment security as a statistician, looking for greater remuneration, according to Ayres.

117 **three inches, what biologists call recruit size:** When razor clam populations are discussed or made into charts, it is typically only recruit-sized clams that are counted.

118 **the department was undercounting:** Ayres, interviews with author, including October 27, 2016; and Scott Mazzone, QIN razor clam manager, interview with author, October 31, 2014. In 2013, the Quinault Indian Nation discovered the error in how WDFW was determining the number of digger trips. That error, in turn, led to an undercounting of the state's harvest in many cases—sometimes by a very small amount but other times by as much as 20 to 30 percent, or even 40 percent. It is not known exactly when this "estimation methodology error" started, but according to Ayres, it occurred as procedures were updated to computer programs and spreadsheets around 1995. In other words, it was a legacy error. It took Ayres only twenty minutes of reviewing to confirm the error after the QIN pointed it out. The state immediately owned up to the mistake and negotiated with the QIN a weighted harvesting schedule for five future years to compensate; that also meant fewer clamming days for the general public at Mocrocks and Copalis. Ironically, in some ways the issue helped reinforce state/tribal cooperation, and the co-management relationship with the tribe is something of a model.

The table detailing the number of digger trips and total harvest, kept continuously by WDFW since 1949, has been retroactively corrected for Long Beach and Twin Harbors to 2004, and for Mocrocks and Copalis to 1997. Correcting this historical *Seasonal Summary of Razor Clam Recreational Harvest* was an arduous task. Much of the data was hard to access, stored in obsolete software and hardware. Data from periods before 1997 are virtually inaccessible. However, Ayres thinks the error does not extend earlier than 1995, and at any rate data from earlier periods, say from the 1980s and before, was calculated in other ways and is considered reliable.

To describe the error in more detail: people arrive at the beach to dig in a bell curve–shaped pattern. The department takes a snapshot of people digging on the beach at a certain time during the low tide and then applies an expansion formula based on that pattern to determine the total number of diggers for the low tide period; the error was in the expansion formula that determined this "creel census." It was not a consistent difference, and the error amount varied each day depending on such variables as when during the low tide the count occurred. Revising the data meant a day-by-day reconstruction of each season at each beach.

119 **knowledgeable, friendly and dedicated—and mistaken:** Matt Winters, "Our Beach Can Sustain a 50-50 Split of Clams," *The Chinook Observer*, July 17, 2013. Matt Winters is editor of *The Chinook Observer*.

120 **subtidal razor clams a different species:** Timothy D. Schink, Katherine A. McGraw, and Kenneth K. Chew, *Pacific Coast Clam Fisheries* (Seattle: Washington Sea Grant Program, College of Ocean and Fishery Sciences, University of Washington, 1983), 10.

120 **have gone to the beach and counted:** Ibid., 13.

121 **when there's time they count the wastage:** Ayres, interview. WDFW razor clam staff regularly try to check a hundred holes at random on the beach for wastage, in between the time-consuming tasks of counting and interviewing clammers during scheduled digs. They stick a shovel in a hole and look around; discarded or damaged clams are generally near the surface. They collect the numbers throughout the season to come up with an average. "It's something we've been doing for a long time," says Ayres.

Recently, wastage rates have been holding stable around 2 to 4 percent, though on any given day the rate might be higher, say 6 percent. Historically, there have been times when the rate spiked much higher, to 22 percent or more, and sometimes the season was closed because of so much wastage. "We don't see that (level of wastage) anymore," says Ayres.

CHAPTER 8. LICENSED TO CARRY

128 **they drop to one knee:** Eileen Crimmin, "Clams! Clams! Clams!" *The Seattle Times*, June 23, 1968.

132 **the clam digger's gun:** P. F. Halferty, "Scenes at Clam Bees in Washington, and P. F. Halferty," *The Seattle Daily Times*, May 16, 1919.

132 **A clam gun is a shovel with sharp edges:** Norah Berg, *Lady on the Beach*, with Charles Samuels (London: Alvin Redman, 1957), 147.

133 **Rules for razor clamming suddenly included the tube:** "Limits and Seasons Listed for Digging Clams," *The Seattle Times*, May 23, 1963. The story reported, "It is lawful to use hands, fork, pick, hattock or shovel, and to employ a cylindrical can or tube."

133 **put away their guns and shovels at noon:** Brad O'Connor, "Lousy Weekend to Be a Clam," *The Seattle Times*, May 6, 1977.

134 **I danced with joy:** Later, I spoke with a researcher at the Seattle patent library, and he told me that he, too, was shocked to have found patents prior to 1976 in recent searches. "It started around two years ago," he said. "Someone's indexing the old records but not telling anyone."

134 **For a living he drove logging trucks:** Jim Batstone's children—Patsy Price, Betsy Batstone-Cunningham, and Jim Ott—as well as relatives including Aven and Shirley Andersen, interviews with the author, October 2016.

134 **created the tube at age thirty-eight:** Lionel R. Patton, "'Clam-Diggers' Sweetheart Is a Real Dandy," *The Sunday Olympian*, May 19, 1957. According to the article, it was a basement workshop, but the family says it was a garage workshop, the lower level of a small, two-story apartment complex.

134 **the clam digger's sweetheart:** One-page flyer, in the razor clam file at the Aberdeen Museum of History. Another flyer, in the family's possession, has the Aberdeen sporting goods store Reiner's advertising the "Sandpiper clam gun"—"the new Clam Gun everyone is talking about"— for $6.75. That's about $60 adjusted to inflation in 2016. According to his children, Batstone didn't mind people making a clam tube for their own use, but he wasn't happy about those who copied his invention and sold it.

138 **making clam shovels in the 1930s:** Scott Wise, True Temper corporate historian, personal communication by email, August 18, 2014. The True Temper corporate website also has historical information on its "About" page; see www.true-temper.com/about/about-true-temper/.

138 **scoop the clam out in a single motion:** Byron Fish, "Clam Guns Come in Many Shapes and Sizes but All Have Faults," *The Seattle Times*, March 9, 1952.

139 **called a "Westport bend" or "Westport hook":** Alan Rammer, WDFW razor clam educator (retired), interview with author, August 17, 2014. Rammer based his understanding from his interviews with old-timers conducted in the 1990s. Rammer's handwritten notes of these interviews are in the razor clam files at the Aberdeen Museum of History.

139 **sold them for $10:** Don Hannula, "Aberdeen Man Dug 1,091 Pounds on One

Tide," *The Seattle Times*, June 21, 1970. Hannula was born in Aberdeen in 1931, and his father, a Finnish immigrant, ran a fish market. Hannula had a personal understanding of the razor clamming and seafood-gatherer way of life, which carried over to his work as a writer and columnist at *The Seattle Times*. In his story, Hannula says, "It was Rhodes who put the 'Westport Hook' (a distinct bend at the top of blade) into the clam gun." By contrast, Norah Berg in *Lady on the Beach* calls the Westport Hook "where the metal joins the wood" (87), meaning the neck of the shovel, but in this she appears to be mistaken.

140 **resemblance to the spit in the boat basin at Westport:** Interview with Irwin Jasper by Alan Rammer, March 1990, in razor clam file at the Aberdeen Museum of History. The Museum of the North Beach's collection includes a Jack Rhodes Westport bend shovel, stamped No. 148.

CHAPTER 9. EATING THEM, AFTER ALL, IS THE POINT

147 **Grizzly bears in Alaska eat Pacific razor clams:** Mothers with their cubs are especially likely to eat razor clams. Grizzlies in general are incredible diggers, with claws and a huge hump of muscle designed for this purpose. Tom S. Smith and Steven T. Partridge, "Dynamics of Intertidal Foraging by Coastal Brown Bear in Southwestern Alaska," *The Journal of Wildlife Management* 68, no. 2 (April 2004): 233–240. Also Dr. Tom S. Smith, wildlife biologist, interview with author, April 25, 2015.

148 **preferred them cooked with no breading:** Gene Woodwick, interview with author, April 17, 2015. From cooking for loggers, Woodwick went on to become a journalist, regional historian, book author, and founding director of the Ocean Shores Interpretive Center.

150 **hard to keep alive during plane flights:** Alan Heather, manager of Quinault Pride Seafood, interview with author, November 5, 2014.

155 **Aberdeen restaurateur named Rube Walden:** Compiled by Karen Barkstrom, "World Gone By," *Aberdeen Daily News*, March 4, 2012.

156 **the best thing to take on an empty stomach:** Razor clam can label, Warrenton Clam Co., Pacific Shellfish Ephemera, Matt Winters Digital Collection.

156 **popular as chasers in the bar:** This claim is according to Lee Marriott, director of the Museum of the North Beach. The museum has a collection of the clear-glass miniature bottles, embossed with "Clam Juice, Sea Beach Packing, Aberdeen, Wash, U.S.A."

156 **The Warrenton cannery extolled its process:** "The Story of Warrenton Clams," Pacific Shellfish Ephemera, Matt Winters Digital Collection.

157 **Norah Berg offered her cooking advice:** Norah Berg, *Lady on the Beach*, with Charles Samuels (London: Alvin Redman, 1957), 152.

CODA

174 **same general police powers as other law enforcement:** In some respects, game wardens have more power, because they have broad inspection authority without a warrant if it appears you've been hunting or fishing and they have reason to believe there's evidence of a violation.

175 **It's all at the judge's discretion:** Joanna Eide, WDFW legal liaison, interview with author, September 17, 2015. Prior to 2012, if you were found to be more than one limit over—that is, had more than thirty clams—a court appearance was mandatory, but if you were less than one limit over—that is, had more than fifteen but fewer than thirty—the penalty was $80 plus $10 for each clam.

176 **waders stuffed with 225 clams:** For stories of poaching, see Herb Williams, *Twin Harbors Tales* (Tacoma: H. Williams, 1967), and Don Hannula, "Aberdeen Man Dug 1,091 Pounds on One Tide," *The Seattle Times*, June 21, 1970. I also received an earful interviewing Alan Rammer, razor clam educator (retired) and Sergeant Matthew Nixon (retired).

178 **on the hard sand of Copalis Beach:** Pacific Northwest Flying.com, www.pacificnorthwestflying.com/index.php.

178 **Don Eastvold was the person responsible:** Gene Woodwick, Washington coast historian and author, interview with author, April 17, 2015.

180 **such as pteropods, a kind of snail:** Craig Welch, "Acidification Already Eating Away at Tiny Creatures along Our Coast," *The Seattle Times*, April 30, 2014.

181 **Die-offs have been observed:** Joe Schumacher, QIN biologist, interview with the author, October 8, 2014. Also see Terri Hansen, "Ocean's Rising Acidification Affecting Shellfish That Coastal Tribes Depend On," on the Indian Country Today Media Network, posted August 14, 2014, http://indiancountrytodaymedianetwork.com/2014/08/14/oceans-rising-acidification-dissolves-shellfish-coastal-tribes-depend-156395.

181 **Clams are a high-protein, low-fat food:** Doris Hicks, interview with author, December 3, 2014. Hicks works at Seafood Health Facts.

181 **when it comes to fetal development:** Kenneth R. Weiss, "Digging for Data," *Los Angeles Times*, July 31, 2006.

182 **umami is the savory taste:** Umami Information Center, www.umamiinfo.com.

183 **a state tree, a state amphibian:** "State Symbols," Washington State Legislature, http://leg.wa.gov/Symbols/pages/default.aspx. Also see "Washington State Symbols, Songs, and Emblems," on the Netstate.com website, www.netstate.com/states/symb/wa_symb.htm.

SELECTED BIBLIOGRAPHY

Alexanderdottir, Marianna, Patrick Cox, and Wendy Beeghley-White. *Washington State Sport Catch Report for Foodfish 1993*. Washington: Department of Fish and Wildlife, 1995.

Anderson, Jason W. "The World Is Their Oyster? Interpreting the Scope of Native American Off-Reservation Shellfish Rights in Washington State." *Seattle University Law Review* 23, no. 145 (1999): 145–73.

Batstone, James. Clam digging device. US Patent 2,802,689, issued August 13, 1957, filed March 30, 1956.

Berg, Norah. *Lady on the Beach*. With Charles Samuels. London: Alvin Redman Limited, 1957.

Capoeman, Pauline K., ed. *Land of the Quinaults*. Taholah: Quinault Indian Nation, 1990.

Coan, Eugene V., Paul Valentich Scott, and Frank R. Bernard. *Bivalve Seashells of Western North America: Marine Bivalve Mollusks from Arctic Alaska to Baja California*. Santa Barbara, CA: Santa Barbara Museum of Natural History, 2000.

Dixon, George. *A Voyage Round the World; but More Particularly to the North-West Coast of America*. London: Geo. Goulding, 1789.

Dyson, Karen, and Daniel D. Huppert. "Regional Economic Impacts of Razor Clam Beach Closures Due to Harmful Algal Blooms (HABS) on the Pacific Coast of Washington." *Harmful Algae* 9 (2010): 264–271.

Feely, Richard A., Terrie Klinger, Jan A. Newton, and Meg Chadsey, eds. *Scientific Summary of Ocean Acidification in Washington State Marine Waters, Washington State Blue Ribbon Panel on Ocean Acidification*, National Oceanic and Atmospheric Organization Oceanic and Atmospheric Research (NOAA OAR), November 2012. Available at https://fortress.wa.gov/ecy/publications/SummaryPages/1201016.html.

Gosling, Elizabeth. *Bivalve Molluscs: Biology, Ecology and Culture*. Oxford, UK: Fishing News Books, 2003.

Hickey, Barbara, Vera Trainer, et al. "A Springtime Source of Toxic Pseudo-Nitzschia

Cells on Razor Clam Beaches in the Pacific Northwest." *Harmful Algae* 25 (May 2013): 1–14.

Hickey, Hannah. "Predicting When Toxic Algae Will Reach Washington and Oregon Coasts." *UW Today*, September 4, 2014, www.washington.edu/news/2014/09/04/predicting-when-toxic-algae-will-reach-washington-and-oregon-coasts/.

Landry, Michael R., and Barbara M. Hickey, eds. *Coastal Oceanography of Washington and Oregon*. Elsevier Oceanography Series 47. Amsterdam: Elsevier Science Ltd, 1989.

Lassuy, Dennis R., and Douglas Simons. *Species Profiles: Life Histories and Environmental Requirements of Coastal Fishes and Invertebrates (Pacific Northwest): Pacific Razor Clam*. Washington, D.C.: National Wetlands Research Center, 1989.

Madsen, Walter M. Clam gun with vent mechanism for easing withdrawal from the sand. Patent 4,244,614, issued January 13, 1981, filed February 1, 1979.

McKellar, Jamie M. "Growth and Maturity of the Pacific Razor Clam in Eastern Cook Inlet, Alaska, A Thesis." Fairbanks, AL: UMI Dissertation Number 1572587, December 2014.

McLachlan, A., and A. C. Brown. *The Ecology of Sandy Shores*, 2nd ed. Burlington, MA: Academic Press, 2006.

McMillin, Harvey C. *The Life-History and Growth of the Razor Clam*. Olympia: State of Washington Department of Fisheries, 1924.

Nickerson, Richard B. *A Critical Analysis of Some Razor Clam (Siliqua patula, Dixon) Populations in Alaska*. Juneau: State of Alaska, Department of Fish and Game, 1975.

Odebrecht, Clarisse, et al. "Surf Zone Diatoms: A Review of the Drivers, Patterns and Role in Sandy Beaches Food Chains." *Estuarine, Coastal and Shelf Science* 150, part A (October 5, 2014): 24–35.

Pacific Shellfish Ephemera, Matt Winters Digital Collection. This is the personal collection of Matt Winters, publisher/editor of the *Chinook Observer*. Contact Matt Winters at mwinters@chinookobserver.com for information and permission to view the online Flickr album.

Puckett, John. Razor clam digger. Patent 3,089,721, issued May 14, 1963, filed December 30, 1960.

Razor Clam, Department of Fisheries and Oceans (DFO), 2001. Razor Clam. DFO Science Stock Status Report C6-15, Canada, 2001. PDF from Canada's Department of Fisheries and Oceans available at www.dfo-mpo.gc.ca/csas/Csas/status/2001/SSR2001_C6-15e.pdf.

Razor Clam Species Profile. Alaska Department of Fish and Game. www.adfg.alaska.gov/index.cfm?adfg=razorclam.

"Razor Clams." Oregon Department of Fish and Wildlife. www.dfw.state.or.us/mrp/shellfish/razorclams/.

"Razor Clams: How Recreational Razor Clam Seasons Are Set." Washington Department of Fish and Wildlife. Available at wdfw.wa.gov/fishing/shellfish/razorclams/seasons_set.html.

Schink, Timothy D., Katherine A. McGraw and Kenneth K. Chew. *Pacific Coast Clam Fisheries*. Seattle: Washington Sea Grant Program, College of Ocean and Fishery Sciences, University of Washington, 1983.

Sigurdson, Clarence. "The History of [the] West Coast Razor Clam Industry." Unpublished typewritten pages. Undated, but circa 1985, in the collection of the Museum of the North Beach, Moclips, Washington.

Smith, Tom S., and Steven T. Partridge. "Dynamics of Intertidal Foraging by Coastal Brown Bears in Southwest Alaska." *The Journal of Wildlife Management*, 68, no. 2 (April 2004): 233–240.

Szarzi, Nicole J., Terrance J. Quinn III, and Douglas N. McBride. "Assessment of Shallow-water Clam Resources: Case Study of Razor Clams, Eastern Cook Inlet, Alaska." *International Council for the Exploration of the Sea (ICES) Marine Science Symposium* 199 (1995): 274–286.

Tegelberg, Herb, and Earl Finn. *The 1963 and 1964 Razor Clam Fisheries*. Olympia: State of Washington Department of Fisheries, 1967.

Tegelberg, Herb, Mike Leboki, and Doug Magoon. *The 1968 Razor Clam Fisheries and Sampling Programs*. Olympia: State of Washington, Department of Fisheries, 1969.

Unruh, Robyn. "History of the World's Largest Frying Pan and Razor Clam Festival." Self-published, Long Beach, WA, 2013, and then updated by Keleigh Schwartz in 2016 and posted on the "History" page of the Long Beach Razor Clam Festival website, http://longbeachrazorclamfestival.com/long-beach-razor-clam-festival-history/.

Weymouth, F. W., H. C. McMillin, and H. B. Holmes. "Growth and Age at Maturity of the Pacific Razor Clam, Siliqua Patula (Dixon)." *Bulletin of the Bureau of Fisheries* XLI, document no. 984 (Washington, D.C.: Government Printing Office, 1925).

Winter, A. G., R. L. H. Deits, D. S. Dorsch, A. H. Slocum, and A. E. Hosoi, "Razor Clam to Roboclam: Burrowing Drag Reduction Mechanism and Their Robotic Adaptation." *Bioinspiration and Biomimetics*, April 8, 2014.

Woodwick, Gene. *Images of America: Ocean Shores*. Charleston, SC: Arcadia Publishing, 2010.

Wyer, Holly. "Pacific Razor Clam." Monterey Bay Aquarium Seafood Watch, March 6, 2013.

INDEX

A

Ackley, Daisy, 79–80
Alaskan razor clams, 106
amnesiac shellfish poisoning (ASP), 101, 102, 189
anatomy of razor clams, 60–64
Andrew, Bob, 25, 26, 28, 131, 132, 142
Atlantic razor clams, 66–67; described, 16; eating, 158
Ayres, Dan, 98, 109–11, 116, 117, 118, 119, 120, 121, 122, 123

B

bag limits, 85–86
Basic Sautéed Razor Clams, 21–22
Batstone, James E., 134–35, 136
beach driving, 36–37, 173–74
beach names, 177–78
Beasley, Dale, 119, 149
Berg, Norah, 77, 78, 132–33, 157–58
bivalves, 61
Blum, Joe, 99
Boldt, Judge George Hugo, 45, 46, 91
Brock's Razor Clams with Black Bean Sauce, 143–45

C

canned razor clams, 75–78, 82, 156–57
Canoe Journey, 44, 45
Chadwick, Dan, 175
Charlie's eatery, Seattle, 86
chart of digger trips 1949–2013, 105*fig.*
Cheng, Henry, 117, 118
Chopped Clams with Miso, 159
chowders, 87, 107–8, 123–26, 154, 155, 169
"clam guns," 127, 128–33, 135–36, 138, 142, 143
"Clamity Fritters," 38–40
clamming: when to go, 19–20
clam nectar, juice, 155–56
clams: razor. *See* razor clams.
"Clamshell Railroad" Clams Chowder, 107
clam shovels, 19*fig.*, 127–42, 163–64
Clams with Snap Peas in Champagne Vinaigrette, 53–54
clam tubes, 128–34, 142, 143; described, 19*fig.*; Sandpiper, 134*fig.*
Clark, William, 24, 58
climate change and ocean acidification, 180–81
Cobain, Kurt, 42
Coconut Milk Curry Clams with Basil, 161
commercial clamming: vs. recreational

215

clamming, 83–84; regulations governing, 89–90
Connor Creek, 32
Copalis Beach, 178–79
counting: clam diggers, 119–20, 188–89; razor clams, 110–5, 117
Cowles, David, 60–61, 62
Cox, Frank, 101
crabs and clams, 119, 149, 150
Croston, George, 82

D

Dahlia Lounge, Seattle, 143
Dan's Low-Fat Razor Clam Chowder, 123–24
Darwin, L. H., 89
Dennis Company, 129–30, 137
Dennis, Randy, 42, 130, 131, 132, 137, 142
Depot Restaurant, Long Beach, 107
diatoms, 55–59
digger trips 1949–2013, 105*chart*
diggers, counting, 120, 188–89
disability licenses, 37
Dixon, George, 74
Do, Loc, 175–76
domoic acid, 101–5, 181, 189
driving on beaches, 173–74

E

earthquakes and tsunamis, 25–26, 179–80
Eastvold, Don, 178–79
ecology of surf-zone, 56–59
Eisenhower, President Dwight D., 45–46
Elston, Ralph, 94–95, 97
Erickson, Arlene, 88

F

Fish, Byran, 138
flying to the beach, 178–79
Frank, Leon, 49, 51

"Fresh Clam Balls," 88
frying pan sculpture in Long Beach, 25*fig.*, 26, 27

G

Gage, Lorenzo R., 82
grizzly bears, 147

H

habitat of razor clams, 34–35
Halferty, Peter F., 75–76, 132, 141, 157
harmful algal blooms (HABs), 104
hatchery-raised razor clams, 93, 96
Heather, Alan, 149–50
Hickey, Barbara, 103
Hicks, Doris, 181
Hollowed, John, 47
Horner, Rita, 103
Hosoi, Anette, 66
hypoxia events, 181

I

Ivar's restaurant, 21

J

Jake, Helene, 79
James, Justine, 47, 52
jewelry, razor clam, 37*fig.*
Johnson, Brock, 143
Johnstone, Ed, 44, 53
Johnston, Greg, 142
Juan de Fuca oceanic plate thrusts, 25–26

K

Kalaloch, 34, 41, 174, 177
Karen (author's wife), 9, 11, 21, 73, 92, 130, 148, 155, 157, 158, 161, 170
Karen's Razor Clam Dip, 170
Katamura, Taichi, 151, 152–53, 159

L

Lady on the Beach (Samuels and Berg), 77, 132–33, 157
Lalewicz, Michael, 107, 108
Lee's Razor Clam Chowder, 124–26
Lewin, Joyce, 56, 57
Lewis, Meriwether, 24, 58
licenses to harvest clams, 92, 171, 187–189, 204
Long Beach, 24–30, 34
Long Beach Razor Clam Festival, 26–30

M

Madsen, Walter M., 137
management areas for razor clam harvesting, 41, 177–78
maps: extent of razor clams, 35*map*; razor clam management area, 43*map*
Marie's "Feed the Crowd" Chowder, 169
Marriott, Lee, 124, 156
Mazzone, Scott, 151
McCausland, Bob, 65, 93, 97, 121
McMillin, Harvey, 55, 58, 64, 66, 76, 121
McDougal, Teri Lee, 33*fig*.
mechanical razor clamming, 82–83
Melville, Herman, 146
Moby-Dick (Melville), 146
Mocrocks management area, 177–78
Monterey Bay Aquarium Seafood Watch, 151
Museum of the North Beach, Moclips, 80, 124, 156

N

New England-style clam chowder, 154
Nikko Restaurant, Seattle, 86
NIX (Nuclear Inclusion Unknown) disease, 95–99, 105, 187–88
Northup, Tom, 94
Northwest Indian Fisheries Commission, 47

O

ocean acidification and climate change, 180–81
Ocean Shores, 30–34
Ocean Shores Razor Clam Festival, 31
O'Connell, Marie, 169

P

Pacific razor clams, 64, 66–67; appearance, anatomy, 15–16; eating, 158; where found, 15
paralytic shellfish poisoning (PSP) testing, 101
Parson, Clayton, 111, 120
phytoplankton, 55–56
Pioneer Brand Clams, 75–76
Pioneer's Sea Beach Packing clam juice, 156
poaching clams, 91, 174–77
Pratt, Al, 139
Pseudo-nitzschia phytoplankton, 103–4
Puckett, John, 136–137
"pumped-area method" of counting clams, 109–16

Q

Quinault Indian Nation (QIN), 42, 43–45, 47–52, 79, 110, 149, 151
Quinault Pride Seafood enterprise, 149–50

R

Rafeedie, Judge Edward, 46, 47, 110
Rammer, Alan, 91–92, 96, 99–100
Razor Clam Canners Association, 81–82, 149
Razor Clam Ceviche, 160
razor clam festival: in Long Beach, 31; in Ocean Shores, 26–30
razor clamming tubes, 84–85
razor clams, 173–74; anatomy of, 60–64;

annual yield, 17; Atlantic, 16, 66–67; bag limits, 85–86; canned, 75–78, 82, 156–57; canning, 155–56; clams with snap peas in champagne vinaigrette (recipe), 53–54; cleaning and keeping, 172–73; counting, 110–17; digging abilities of, 66–70; dressing, 146–47, 148; eating, 146–58; enforcement of regulations, 174–77; growth study of, 117–18; habitat, 34–35; hatchery-raised, 93, 96; jewelry, 37*fig.*; licenses to harvest, 86, 92, 171, 187–89; management areas for harvesting, 41; nutrition and harm, 181; Pacific, 16, 64, 66–67; personal-use regulations, 1929–2016, 185–86; poaching clams, 91, 175–77; postcard in shape of, 81*fig.*; recipes. *See* recipes; recreational vs. commercial clamming, 83–84; regulations governing, 18, 104, 171–77; reproduction of, 60; sculptures, 31–33; seasons, 18; shells, fun with, 183; steaming, 182; as sushi, 152–53

Reagan, President Ronald, 46

recipes: Basic Sautéed Razor Clams, 21–22; Brock's Razor Clams with Black Bean Sauce, 143–45; Chopped Clams with Miso, 159; "Clamity Fritters," 38–40; "Clamshell Railroad" Clams Chowder, 107; Clams with Snap Peas in Champagne Vinaigrette, 53–54; Coconut Milk Curry Clams with Basil, 161; Dan's Low-Fat Clam Chowder, 123–24; "Fresh Clam Balls," 88; Karen's Fry Mix, 73; Karen's Razor Clam Dip, 170; Lee's Razor Clam Chowder, 124–26; list of recipes, 193; Marie's "Feed the Crowd" Chowder, 169; Q&A, 181–82; Razor Clam Ceviche, 160; Sautéed Razor Clams in Brown Butter, 22; Sautéed Razor Clams with Capers, 23; Silvey Family Fried Razor Clams, 71–72; Vintage Chowder, 87

recreational vs. commercial clamming, 83–84

regulations governing razor clams, 18, 104, 171–77, 185–87

reproduction of razor clams, 60

Rhodes, Jack, 139–40

O'Connell, Marie, 169

Rich and Will (O'Connell), 162–68

Richard and Colette (motel owners), 100

Rickard, Neil, 96

Rosander, Francis, 79

S

Samuels, Charles, 77

Sandpiper clam tube, 134–35

Sautéed Razor Clams in Brown Butter, 22

Schaefer, Charles, 56, 57

sculptures, 36–37; Long Beach skillet, 25*fig.*, 25–27; Ocean Shores' razor clam, 31–33, 33*fig.*; razor clam in Long Beach, 25*fig.*

"seagulling," 50

Sears, Dann, 84–85

"Shellfish Proviso" in Stevens Treaties, 46–47

shells, fun with, 183

shovels, clam, 127–42

Sigurdson, Clarence, 80

Silvey, Mike, Bebe, and Greg, 71

Silvey Family Fried Razor Clams, 71–72

Simons, Doug, 91, 99

skillet sculpture in Long Beach, 25*fig.*, 26, 27

Skow, Gary, 101

Smith, Jared, 132

steaming clams, 181–82

Stevens, Isaac, 45
Sushi Kappo Tamura, Seattle, 151, 159

T

Thompson, Marilyn, 36, 38
tides, 1, 19–20, 28, 30, 48, 49–50, 64, 77, 78, 104, 119, 147, 173–74
Tinker, Henry, 25
Trainer, Vera, 103
True Temper shovels, 130, 138, 141
tsunamis and earthquakes, 25–26, 179–80

U

umami, 182
United States v. Washington, 45–47, 91, 111

V

Vintage Chowder, 87
violations, infractions of the law, 174–77

W

Walden, Rube, 155
Washington State: razor clam personal-use regulations, 1929–2016, 185–86
Washington State clam, 183
Washington State fisheries: and clamming regulations, 89–90
Westport hook clam shovels, 139–40
Winter, Amos, 66
Winter, Donald, 56, 57 Woodwick, Gene, 147–48

ACKNOWLEDGMENTS

I am indebted to those who shared their expertise and experiences. Biologists, researchers, museum directors, chefs, librarians, legions of razor clammers, and many others were more than generous with their time, insights, and stories. Without their help this book would not have been possible

At the Washington Department of Fish and Wildlife, I'm especially grateful to coastal shellfish manager Dan Ayres, biologist and educator Alan Rammer (retired), and scientific technician Clayton Parson for their unfailing help and readiness to answer my many questions, as well as Officer Loc Do, Sergeant Matt Nixon (retired), Captain Dan Chadwick, scientific technician Zachary Forster, and attorney Joanna Eide.

At Long Beach, Mayor Bob Andrew, Randy Dennis, David Compiche (of the Shelburne Inn), and Carol Zahorsky helped me to understand the Long Beach Peninsula.

In the Ocean Shores area, historian and author Gene Woodwick, motel proprietors Richard and Colette Sexton, and Museum of the North Beach directors Kelly Calhoun and Lee Marriott were likewise indispensable.

At the Quinault Indian Nation, I'm grateful to Justine James, Ed Johnstone, Joe Schumacker, Scott Mazzone, Alan Heather, Pearl Capoeman Baller, and digger Leon Frank; and for further illuminating tribal treaty rights, John Hollowed, with the Northwest

Indian Fisheries Commission, and Phil Katzen, a lead attorney in the Rafeedie case.

Dissecting a clam with Professor David Cowles was eye opening. Fishery biologist Dr. Ralph Elston, biomathematics professor Terrance Quinn, and astronomy professor Woodruff "Woody" Sullivan gave insight into shellfish diseases, wildlife population counts, and ocean tides, respectively.

Jerry Borchert, Frank Cox (retired), Blaine Roberts, and Donn Moyer at the Washington Department of Health illuminated the world of marine toxins; researchers Dr. Vera Trainer, Dr. Stephanie Moore, and Professor Barbara Hickey illuminated the algal blooms that produce them.

Razor clam managers Matt Hunter in Oregon and Carol Kervliet in Alaska detailed stewarding the razor clam resource in their respective states. The Batstone family, including daughters Patsy Price and Betsy Batstone-Cunningham, provided family photographs and memories of Jim Batstone and his razor clam tube invention.

I'm appreciative to all the people who shared ideas about preparing razor clams, including chef Taichi Kitamura (Sushi Kappo Tamura restaurant), Mike and Bebe Silvey, Greg Silvey, Ted Studevant, Amy Spangler, Carol Linn, chef Michael Lalewicz (The Depot restaurant) and chef Brock Johnson (Dahlia Lounge restaurant).

The institutions that house and make available documents, books, artifacts, and historical records were invaluable and made possible the primary research. Kelly Calhoun and Lee Marriott at the Museum of the North Beach in Moclips—still excited about our discovery of a Jack Rhodes Westport-bend shovel in their midst—provided many historical materials and photographs from their razor clam archives. Thanks also to director Abram (Dann) Sears and the Aberdeen Museum of History, with its files of razor clam materials; Louise Richards and the University of Washington Library; as well as the Aberdeen Timberland Library, Ocean Shores Interpretive Center, and Seattle Public Library.

On the editorial side, I extend my warm appreciation to Regan Huff at the University of Washington Press for coaxing the text into something much improved, and to copyeditor Emily Park. Thanks also to Ashley Ahearn and the Society of Environmental Journalists, which helped create the opportunity for this book, and to Sibyl James, Lezlie Jane, Jamie Garner, and Ken Kamber for reading drafts and making suggestions. Alexander Gillis and Gail Workman helped with graphics, and Cynthia Hall made the maps.

Special thanks to Rich, Amy, Erin, and Will O'Connell for the opportunity to join their family at the beach. And I owe a large debt of gratitude to Karen for her support, help with recipes, and enthusiasm for razor clams.

The book drew on these people, and more, and I am grateful to all.

ABOUT THE AUTHOR

DAVID BERGER has worked as arts critic for the *Seattle Times*, executive director of a botanical garden, and communications officer affiliated with a World Heritage Site on the Silk Road in China. He is a recipient of a Metcalf Fellowship for Marine and Environmental Reporting, and his work has appeared in the *Portland Oregonian*, *Travel & Leisure* magazine, and *Black Earth Institute Literary Journal*. David lives in Seattle and when not writing or razor clamming is also a visual artist.